THE FOUNDATION OF
THE CHRISTIAN FAITH

THE FOUNDATION OF THE CHRISTIAN FAITH

A Book for Honest Thinkers, whether Jews or Christians

by

A. LUKYN WILLIAMS, D.D.

Hon. Canon of Ely

WIPF & STOCK · Eugene, Oregon

Wipf and Stock Publishers
199 W 8th Ave, Suite 3
Eugene, OR 97401

The Foundation of the Christian Faith
A Book for Honest Thinkers, whether Jews or Christians
By Williams, A. Lukyn
Softcover ISBN-13: 978-1-6667-3424-9
Hardcover ISBN-13: 978-1-6667-2989-4
eBook ISBN-13: 978-1-6667-2990-0
Publication date 8/19/2021
Previously published by W. Heffer & Sons Ltd., 1943

This edition is a scanned facsimile of
the original edition published in 1943.

Preface

I DESIRE to express my grateful thanks to my son for allowing me to reprint Chapter IX, and especially to my friends the Rev. R. S. Cripps, B.D., author of the well-known Commentary on the Book of Amos, and the Rev. W. Newton Flew, D.D., Vice-Principal of Wesley House, for reading between them the whole manuscript, and making very valuable suggestions. Dr. C. G. Montefiore and Mr. Herbert Loewe, Reader in Rabbinics in the University, have also been most kind in giving me information on one or two points about which I have consulted them. But the whole plan and argument, and method of the book is, I believe, original, and, in any case, I am alone responsible for all it contains.

A L. W.

Cambridge.

By the same Author

Ecclesiastes. Cambridge Bible for Schools and Colleges.

Galatians. Cambridge Greek Testament for Schools and Colleges.

Colossians and *Philemon.* Cambridge Greek Testament for Schools and Colleges.

Justin Martyr, The Dialogue with Trypho: Translation and Notes. 1930.

A Manual of Christian Evidences for Jewish People (a detailed examination of the *Chizzuk Emunah*, 1911, 1919).

The Hebrew–Christian Messiah. (The Warburton Lectures for 1911–1915.)

Mishna, Berakoth. Translation and Notes. 1921.

Talmudic Judaism and Christianity. 1933.

To be published shortly by the Cambridge University Press:—

Adversus Judaeos: A bird's-eye view of Christian Apologiae until the Renaissance.

Contents

		PAGE
PREFACE		iii
INTRODUCTION		vii

First Part.
ISRAEL.

CHAP.		
I.	THE PROMISE TO ABRAHAM	1
II.	THE PRESENT DISTRESS; WHAT REMEDY IS THERE?	7
III.	THE PURPOSE OF THE OLD TESTAMENT	15

Second Part.
JESUS OF NAZARETH.

IV.	THE RECORDS; THE MIRACLES	33
V.	JESUS, HIS LIFE IN GENERAL	38
VI.	THREE TRAITS IN HIS LIFE	44
VII.	THE KINGDOM OF HEAVEN	56
VIII.	THE FOURTH GOSPEL AS THE CONSIDERED FAITH OF CHRISTIANS	69
IX.	THE ATTRACTION OF THE LORD JESUS CHRIST FOR A BELIEVER TO-DAY	83

Third Part.
DIFFICULTIES AND QUESTIONS.

X.	THE TRINITY IN UNITY	97
XI.	THE INCARNATION	107

CONTENTS

CHAP		PAGE
XII.	THE NON-OBSERVANCE OF THE LAW—IN GENERAL	112
XIII	THE NON-OBSERVANCE OF THE LAW—IN CERTAIN DETAILS	129
	(1) Circumcision.	
	(2) Sabbath.	
	(3) The Dietary Laws.	
XIV.	QUESTIONS	137
	(1) Baptism	
	(2) The Lord's Supper.	

APPENDICES.

A.	ST. PAUL	143
B.	JEW or CHRISTIAN	147
NOTES		149
INDICES		
I.	General	162
II.	Biblical	165

INTRODUCTION

I AM told that the average young Englishman who is not a Jew is not likely to buy this book. If so, he is making a mistake, a great mistake; for he will discover in it much that he will find useful, and not a little that interests him.

He may, however, reply that it is written especially for Jews, and that he has no use for Jews, and does not intend to trouble himself with arguments that may well appeal to them; for he himself does not care for reasons adduced from old-time sources. He is concerned with the present, and holds that the claims of Christianity must chiefly, though perhaps not quite entirely, be drawn from its power for work to-day, and even its attitude towards present-day problems. Quite frankly, I grant that there is a great deal in what he says. If Christianity has no word for the present time, and no power to carry out in the lives of its followers its own message, it is worthless, and may safely be set aside as an old-world fable, interesting only to the antiquarian and the student of folk-lore.

But is this so? A candid enquirer into life as we know it is bound to include the fact that there have been in our own day, and still are (though one is chary of placing a final verdict on any one until he is dead), saints, holy men or holy women, equal in holiness of life and sympathetic energy for the well-being of other people, to the saints and holy men or women of any age. What, for instance, of the Sadhu, Sundar Singh, whose life has been written by Canon Streeter and Dr. Appasamy? What of Kagawa of Japan, working with his wife under the most awful conditions in the slums of Kobe, that he might win the very lowest of his people, and also improve the environment of the poor? What of C. T. Studd, the Cambridge cricketer, who gave up all he had (and he was a rich man) that he might bring Chinese and Africans to the true knowledge of God? What of the late Lord Halifax, with his high standard of uprightness, and his devotion to truth, respected and beloved of all men, however much they might differ from him doctrinally? What about Sister Eva of Germany, the modern St. Teresa, though a Lutheran, who, with surpassing humility and absence of egotism, founded sisterhood after sisterhood to benefit the sick and the ignorant and the young? I suppose there never was an age when the power and the influence of our Faith was in greater evidence than to-day.

And yet, and indeed just because of this, it is all the more necessary to know and examine the basis on which it rests. What is the basis of our Faith? What is the one and only reason why we ought to accept the message of Christianity whole-heartedly? This is the question which this book sets itself to answer.

Many men to-day think about religion, and wish to be honest in their thinking. They wish, that is to say, to shirk no real difficulty, and to make no unfair assumption. Naturally they must make three assumptions, for these are inherent in every religion. First,

INTRODUCTION ix

God exists, and takes an interest in us. Secondly, the world exists, and we have to do with it. Thirdly, I, the reader, exist. These three assumptions which, as philosophers tell us, logic can neither prove nor disprove, are the only assumptions made in this book.

No, there is one other, if it can be called an "assumption," for unlike those three it can be verified by any one who will take the time, and it is this: The report of Jesus of Nazareth in the three Gospels (Matthew, Mark, Luke) is trustworthy, generally speaking. Observe that I say, "generally speaking." For no assumption of inspiration is made. Inspiration is a subject for the believer, not for the enquirer, and *for our purpose* is of little importance. Common sense and the ordinary canons of literature are enough to assure us, that, whatever may be the case with the details, the general account of Jesus of Nazareth as recorded in the Gospels may be trusted.

The reader, however, of this book will wish to know for whom it is intended, since to say that it is "for honest thinkers" is too wide a definition. Is it? It has been chosen with some care. It is meant to include all such persons of whatever creed they may be as are enquiring at all into the truth of Christianity. Originally, indeed, the book was intended chiefly for one such set of readers, and was in fact the result of many years of thought about them. For the spare hours of a busy life have largely been given to the study of Judaism, and in particular to those many works of Christian "Apologists" who desired either directly to win Jews to Christ or at least to defend themselves and others from the arguments adduced by

Jews. At all events, every decade or so until the Renaissance saw the production of some such an "Apology," and although, no doubt, many have utterly perished, and many others still exist in manuscript only, at least fifty are accessible to-day in print. I began to study these in the hope of finding arguments on the Christian side which deserved to be drawn up from the waters of Lethe into which they had long since fallen. And such useful arguments do exist. But, as a whole, the result of the study has been very disappointing. The outlook of both Christians and Jews has changed so much that almost all the arguments of the old literature have lost their force, save perhaps among those members of the Jewish race who have no real knowledge of European culture. But this culture is becoming in increasing measure the possession of younger Jews. To them this book was originally addressed, and this accounts for its general contents and arrangement.

Yet the more I have considered the matter the more convinced I have become that there are many Christians, especially among the younger members of the community, who are no longer prepared to accept the Christian Faith unless they themselves have learned how and why it deserves their acceptance. They want to be certain. They wish to know the real basis on which our Faith rests. They are tired of arguments which try to prove that the Bible must be accurate because it is divinely inspired, and that, therefore, we must pin our faith to what it says and follow out its orders. And, on the other hand, they resent the claim to authority on the part of their elders and teachers, however venerable and however highly organized they may be, and they believe that they themselves are quite capable of making for themselves so momentous a decision as the acceptance of the Christian Faith. And in this, at least, they are right.

Thus it is also for such young and honest thinkers that this book is written. Nor do they lose anything by the form in which it was first composed. On the contrary, they gain. For it has been the weakness of many books of Evidences for Christian readers that the writers have never faced the fact that the leaders of the Jewish nation rejected our Lord. Hence the readers of those books have always had at the back of their minds a dim feeling of dissatisfaction. "It is all very well," they would say to themselves, "to try to convince us of the truth of Christianity, but if it be true—Why did the leaders of the Jews not accept it?" They want to know the reason why these leaders rejected our Lord. One answer has always been: Because He claimed to be the Son of God. No! That was an excuse, not the reason. Another answer has also been given: The Jews were expecting a different kind of a Messiah, one who would conquer the whole world and reign as the King of the Jews. No! That answer is quite insufficient.

Why then did the leaders of the Jews reject our Lord? Let me ask another question: Why did they reject John the Baptist?

First Part.

ISRAEL.

Son, thou art ever with Me,
and all that is Mine is thine.

To the Elder Brother.

CHAPTER I.

THE PROMISE TO ABRAHAM.

Now the LORD said unto Abram, Get thee out of thy country, and from thy kindred, and from thy father's house, unto the land that I will shew thee · and I will make of thee a great nation, and I will bless thee, and make thy name great; and be thou a blessing. and I will bless them that bless thee, and him that curseth thee will I curse: and in thee shall all the families of the earth be blessed (Gen. xii. 1–3).

Few people will be prepared to deny that this is one of the most extraordinary promises ever made, alike in itself and in its fulfilment. Observe that the question of the date at which it was given hardly affects its importance. If it were made at some time about B.C 2000, no more need be said. Or if, as some suppose, it was not written down (speaking euphemistically) until the sixth or even the fifth century before the common era, it remains still a promise of almost unique magnitude, for very little of its fulfilment had taken place then. It was no *ex post facto* prophecy.

What a strange promise it was to give! Abraham seems to have been a well-to-do man at the time, still living in that Ur of the Chaldees whose buildings of that day, or earlier, have now been uncovered for us. But the LORD[1] bade him leave. Abraham obeyed the command, and moved to Haran, a city where his father Terah would find the same worship of the heathen deity, the Moon god (Sîn), as prominent as in Ur. How it was that Abraham had ceased to worship idols we cannot guess. Had he already suffered for his faith, as the old legend tells us,[2] we know not, but there must have already been something remarkable about him for God thus to have chosen him. *Get thee out* from all dear to thee, into utterly fresh surroundings, without any certainty whither I shall lead thee. Then, childless though thou art, thy descendants shall become a great nation. Thy own reputation shall be great. Thou thyself shalt be blessed, and thou shalt also be a blessing to others. Yes, even the treatment of thy descendants shall be a touchstone for others of blessing or of woe. But indeed all peoples in the whole wide world shall be blessed in thee.

What a stupendous promise—in width of space and in length of time!

Has the promise been fulfilled? History gives no uncertain reply. For no historian will deny that, whatever the cause, both parts of the promise have been and are being fulfilled in an extraordinary degree.

Yet what of the threat contained in the passage? The LORD said: *Him that curseth thee will I curse*, *i.e.* they who treat Abraham's descendants ill shall suffer for doing so. Is this so? Has this threat been carried out? The Pharaoh of the Exodus indeed suffered. Yet the objection may be raised that the promise to Abraham was a polite fiction, composed

later than B.C. 1450, or, if the Exodus were later, than
B.C. 1250. Sennacherib, the inheritor of blood-thirsty
warfare against Israel, and himself ready to act on the
lines of his predecessors, fled in terror to his own
country, and eventually perished miserably by his
sons' hands. Nor did the dynasty of Nebuchadnezzar
and the Babylonian Empire fare much better. For
it fell only some fifty years after the sack of Jerusalem.
But the most striking examples of the fulfilment of
God's threat of judgment on those who "curse"
Israel belong to modern history. The fate of Spain is
a byword. Nothing could have been more foolish if
earthly prosperity were to be considered than her
expulsion of the Jews in 1492. And Russia! We all
know *Punch's* cartoon, when the pogroms began in
1886, of the ghost of Pharaoh standing before the
Czar, and bidding him Beware. Not always immediately, indeed, but very surely does punishment come
on those who ill-treat the Jews. Herr Adolf Hitler
is no reader of history or he would have remembered
its lessons. This part of the promise to Abraham has
been fulfilled again and again, and I at least believe
that it is certain to be fulfilled in the future.

If, however, the threat in the LORD's words to
Abraham has been, is being, and will be fulfilled,
what shall we say of the promised blessing? This,
that it has already surpassed all possible expectation
on the part of either Abraham or Moses or the writers
of Old Testament times. Anything lower than religion
is, no doubt, difficult to appraise. But it was hardly
an accident that Cyrus, who furthered the expectations
of the Jews, himself prospered, or that Alexandria,

where Jews possessed a high status from the first, became a very great city. Nor can it have been accidental that so long as the Jews were honoured in Spain she retained her greatness, nor that Amsterdam was benefited by the influx of Jewish immigrants after their banishment from the Peninsula.

Has, again, England lost anything by her kindly reception of the Jews from the time of Cromwell onwards? Is her general prosperity since those days a mere matter of chance? Can the long series of Jewish savants, financiers, etc., have proved other than beneficial to those lands which have welcomed their aid? History proclaims its answer in no uncertain voice.[3]

But naturally we think chiefly of religion. How far is true religion due to the descendants of Abraham? How far, and in what way? In every way, and as far as religion has as yet gone. For it is a platitude to remind ourselves that both Christianity and Mohammedanism are the daughters of the religion of Israel, and though Islam is but a step-daughter, and has been accepted (speaking generally) only by the children of Ishmael, the repudiated son of Abraham, yet the former is the basis on which modern civilization rests.

The promise, *In thee shall all the families of the earth be blessed*,[4] was made to Abraham, but it is not possible that he could in the least have understood much of what it implied. His acquaintance with the spaces of earth was very limited; his guesses of time were almost infinitesimal. But now, after some four thousand years since his days, what do we see? The

LORD whom he worshipped, whose orders he obeyed, is known by name throughout the earth, and it is hardly too much to say that all civilized peoples profess to serve Him. Their worship is but imperfect, no doubt; and their service is too often only lip-service, especially in their actions as nations. But they comprise millions of true servants of the LORD, who have placed themselves deliberately at His disposal, bowing down to Him in heart and soul, yielding, so far as they know how, every power of mind and body to do His will. We cannot exaggerate the stupendous character of the present fulfilment of the promised blessing.

Those persons who talk glibly of excising the influence of Jews and their books do not understand what they say. To be sure, there are some sciolists who speak of the Lord Jesus as not being a Jew at all but an Aryan; but this is folly, due to sheer ignorance and prejudice. Jesus of Nazareth was Jewish, brought up in a Jewish environment, and He handed on to us the religion of His forefathers according to the flesh. He was, as the New Testament records tell us, a son of Abraham So that it cannot be reckoned unjustifiable for us Christians to go a step further than we have already gone in our treatment of the promise to Abraham, and to find enclosed within it special reference to Jesus and His work.

For, however we may regard Him, there is no doubt that it is through Him that the nations in general have learned of the LORD who spake to Abraham. Almost all (perhaps quite all) the writers of the New Testament were descendants of Abraham, as were the writers of the Old Testament, so far as we know. We Christians, therefore, owe everything to Israel, and exalt the LORD, who gave His promise to Abraham, and has been fulfilling it in ever-increasing measure. Marvellous indeed is it that from Abraham should spring seed, as it were the sand of the sea for multitude, with blessing to all the nations!

CHAPTER II.

THE PRESENT DISTRESS; WHAT REMEDY IS THERE?

YET although so much blessing has come to the world through Israel, no one can say that her own state corresponds at the present time to what might have been expected. We should have supposed that a nation which has brought to us all so many benefits, both material and spiritual, would itself be in honour and visible prosperity. But this is not the case. It never, indeed, possessed more than a small territory to call its own, which itself was little other than a subject state from about 650 B.C. onwards, and definitely subject for a hundred years or so before the disaster of A.D. 70, when Jerusalem was destroyed and the nation dispersed. Since then the Jews have had no home, save in name and in claim, but have been wanderers throughout the world, some settling here, and some there; here, harried and persecuted to the death; there, preserved rather jealously as the means of worldly wealth. But they never have been able to call a country their own, but have been driven from place to place. Since 1917, indeed, their Holy Land of Palestine has been reckoned in international language as a Home. Perhaps at first England intended to make Palestine their real home, but found it impossible to carry out all she hoped to do. But perhaps her statesmen did realize from the first that all they could give the Jews was the opportunity to make good their national Home in Palestine, and everything depended on their readiness to live up to it. In any case, England has been obliged to be content with encouraging a certain proportion of Jews to live there, and to develop the country, which they are doing in an extraordinary degree and with amazing rapidity.

Be that as it may, of the sixteen millions or so of Jews at the present time, only about two hundred thousand are in Palestine,[1] and the rest are in much the same position as they have been for centuries. A few are very rich, some quite well-to-do, a good many able to live in comparative comfort, and the great majority of them very poor indeed; and, whether rich or poor, they are allowed to reside in the different lands of their Dispersion only at the pleasure of the Gentile nations among whom they live. And, further, the events of the last few years have shown that in these so-called civilized days Jews may be expatriated, persecuted, hounded to death, and even deliberately murdered, for no real crime or misbehaviour—not, it is true, "butchered to make a Roman holiday," but only to make a ladder by which a political party may rise to power.

What remedy can be found? What can be done? Nothing at all, reply many devout Jews, nothing at all, until it pleases the LORD Himself to put forth His power, and, releasing us from our exile, bring us back by His own Almighty hand once more into Palestine.

Let us then be patient, waiting for Him. Surely a right and truly religious spirit, as far as it goes. Endurance in the name of the LORD, and quiet trust in Him, have always been part of the duty and privilege of His servants.

Yet once upon a time there was a great nation, a great Gentile nation, great in science, art, music, literature and war, which had become disheartened. It was thoroughly disappointed. For, after long and painful preparation, at the cost of no little self-sacrifice of time and energy and money, it had attempted to make good its claim to greatness by a war expected to give it world-wide supremacy. Surely this was no selfish motive—as men reckon selfishness. For what could be better for the world in general than to come under the wings of the Eagle, to share in the privileges of true *Kultur?* Strangely and short-sightedly the world in general did not see the fair vision with those imperial eyes, and every other nation preferred to live its own life, and develop itself on its own lines, and even dared to unite with all others against the claim of that great nation. And to her amazement and disgust they were successful. They could not indeed but admire the way in which she, with one strange ally, stood out against the world. But the effort was useless. She was crushingly defeated, and it was only by the forbearance of the enemy, by the devout Christianity of the *Generalissimo* of the allied armies, that the very capital of that nation was not destroyed. For by that time the Air Force of its foes had her country at its mercy.

Twelve years or so passed by. The nation became

increasingly despondent. Failure had been written over all her efforts. Her sufferings had been in vain; her efforts useless.

And then came a Man! You are indeed a great nation, he told them. A great nation? Nay, the greatest of all the nations; greatest in virile strength; greatest in intellectual ability; greatest in the fineness of your purpose; greatest in your moral aims! You are but suffering from an inferiority complex, wholly unjustified. Awake! Awake! Be united, class with class, rich with poor, and reject from among you every strange element. There are those dwelling in your midst who do not belong to you, and are but parasites, living by and on you, by and on you who are the true nobility of earth! Treat them like parasites, exterminate them, or at least expel them, and if any do remain, as such creatures will, keep them in their proper place, able to eke out for themselves a bare existence, and even this at your expense. Take up, I say, your right position! Arise in your true character! Be true Germans, the finest flower of God's creation!

And the nation responded. "Am I a Nazi? I? Ja!" cried the girl joyfully. For she had felt the revival throbbing through her veins, and she was typical of German youth and manhood. The Appeal succeeded, and to-day Germany is wholly different in hope and energy and glad expectation of brilliant success in the near future. The depression has vanished; her inferiority complex is gone; her self-reliance has returned. Her citizens once more deny themselves. They are willing to go to any extreme in furthering their nation's cause. "Awake! Awake!" And she is awake, as never before.

No one has ever made that appeal to the Jews, and I pray God that no one ever may. For Jews are meant for better things than that. When I say "no one," I naturally mean no one possessing the same great oratorical powers and the dominant personality of the Führer. Josephus may describe with intense self-satisfaction his own exploits in the revolt that led to the calamity of A.D. 70, but no one has ever suspected Josephus of greatness. Barcochba may have been a worthy man in his own way, but we know almost nothing about him, although he was the nominal head in the last disastrous uprising against Hadrian in A.D. 132. Shabbethai Zevi in the seventeenth century would call the nation together, but his movement collapsed when he accepted Islam. Theodore Herzl in the closing years of the nineteenth century had a fine cry of Back to the Land, but his mere secular Zionism was rightly suspected by Achad Ha'am[2] of failing to give that heart satisfaction which the nation needed, for intellectual vigour and material success are not sufficient.

Yet there was one person who made an almost successful appeal to his nation. In the third decade of our era appeared on the confines of the wilder parts of Judaea, somewhere on the banks of Jordan, a man who summoned the Jewish nation to arise from its apathy, and held out to them the hope of a speedy deliverance. For they needed the message. Troops of their imperial master were on the move throughout the land, and the agents of Rome were collecting everywhere the taxes she had imposed upon it. The people were disheartened; for there seemed to be no escape from this bitter servitude to heathens whom they rightly despised, in spite of their magnificence and material power. But John the Baptizer called aloud, and the Jewish populace flocked from all parts to hear him. We can hardly be wrong in assuming him to have said, "Now is your opportunity; you may be free; you can be free; if you do but listen to my words and act upon them. For your freedom depends on this condition."

What then was his message? It was not like the Führer's. Nay, it was the very antithesis to that. For it was the same message that was sent to Israel of old, whenever the nation found itself in distress, trampled under the heels of a foreign foe. One message, and one only, was ever recurrent on the lips of the ancient teachers, and it was summed up in God's word to Joshua: *Get thee up; wherefore art thou thus fallen upon thy face? Israel hath sinned . . . therefore the children of Israel cannot stand before their enemies* (Joshua vii. 10–12. *Cf.* Judges ii. 11–18; vi. 1, 7–10).

It was this message, and no other, with modifications of thought and expression due to the period, which John the Baptizer proclaimed. And the populace heard him gladly, pledging themselves, by a not unnatural sign, that they would leave their sins and turn to the LORD, cleansed for His service.

The message was not, you will notice, You Jews are a fine race, the finest of all races, the very seed of Abraham, God's friend; therefore arise in your strength and all will soon be well. It was not that. It was: *Repent;* change your mind, not about the relation of yourselves to other nations, but about your own attitude towards God. Get right with God. Down, down on your knees before Him, that He may raise you up.

With the populace in general his appeal succeeded; but not with the titular king, or the aristocracy, or the ecclesiastics—Sadducees and Pharisees, Priests and Scribes, the leaders of the nation. Why was this?

It is easy enough to see why Herod Antipas rejected John the Baptist, and even put him to death. *Jeshurun waxed fat and kicked* is a true proverb. Prosperous and successful people do not like being found fault with; and when John rebuked the king for marrying his brother's wife he put him in prison. For he was no David that he should suffer his inferiors to tell him the truth. Possibly indeed, he ordered the imprisonment from a wish to keep John safe from Herodias' fury, but if so she was too clever for the crafty king. When she had her chance she took it, and by a trick got the Baptist's head brought to her on a dish—fit for the birthday feast.[3]

Herod Antipas' rejection of John the Baptist's message we can all understand. But why did the leaders of the Jews reject it? There were the Sadducees, priestly and aristocratic, some worldly, others (it would seem) very conservative in their treatment of the Law of Moses as it stood, not admitting any development in its interpretation. Why did they reject John's message?

There were also the Pharisees, the growing party in

religion, men not hampered by fossilized exposition, yet quite sincere in their religion. For it is only a vulgar error to suppose that when Jesus used the Greek word "hypocrites" it meant at that time what we mean by it to-day.[4] No doubt they "put all their goods in their windows." No doubt they did wish their religious excellence to be known, but (with some exceptions) they were not Pecksniffs. Sincere and honourable men as they were, Why did they reject the message of John the Baptizer? Why?

The answer lies in what has already been hinted at, the oneness of John's message with that of the prophets of old. But this is a subject which cannot be adequately considered with a passing reference, but requires a chapter to itself. For the message of John the Baptist was in the proper line of the cry of God's earlier messengers.

CHAPTER III.

THE PURPOSE OF THE OLD TESTAMENT.

WHAT is the purpose of the writers of the Old Testament if it be not to record the training of a chosen people, that first the people, and then all the nations of the world through them, may learn what God expects and enables men to be?

If this is so we may not define off-hand either what God wants, or how He will achieve His aim. We can but trace out the facts given us in the Scriptures which He has caused to be written, and therefore has "inspired" in some sense of the word.

But "inspired" has many connotations, and every reader of the Bible, if he be uninstructed, is sure that he knows what "inspiration" includes. I myself do not profess to know either its extent or its method. God caused the Scriptures to be written, as has been said, that Israel, and through Israel the Gentiles, might learn God's will, and, grasping His intention and receiving His help, might attain to the performance of that will.

This was the purpose of the Old Testament writings; everything else being subordinated to this. History, of course, there is, but it is didactic history. The historians trace out the relation of the LORD to His people, His encouragement of their well-doing and His discipline of them when they have done ill; and, yet again, His blessing when they have turned back to Him in repentance and humble faith.

Poetry, and the sublimest poetry, there is also, but the poets were all doing their best to describe the LORD and His work for men. They pour out of their very hearts their assurance of His care for themselves and their nation, and, lamenting their own and the nation's sins, describe in pathetic and anxious strains the need of repentance, and the gracious willingness of the LORD to pardon.

Thus the historians and the poets are at one in endeavouring to deepen in the nation the sense of the moral and spiritual claims of the LORD upon them.

Priests also there were, men deeply impressed by the awfulness of the LORD, and the need for the utmost strictness of form and rite in His worship. How much part, however, the priests as such took in the process of seeing with increasing clearness the spiritual demands of the LORD, and setting their visions before the people, is uncertain. It is a common assumption that the priests were essentially conservative, and were generally satisfied with the punctilious performance of their sacred duties. Yet this is more than doubtful. For, as we remember that oriental nations always read symbolism into everything, and therefore quite naturally clothe spiritual truths in symbolic terms, it is difficult to suppose that the minute regulations of the worship (for example) were not intended from the very first to be symbolical of the need for holiness on the part of the worshippers of the LORD. In other words, probably the author or authors of the Pentateuch were already impressed with a sense of His ethical demands upon those who professed to serve Him, and they may have had this impression from quite early times.

Be that as it may with regard to the priests, there is no doubt at all about the prophets. Their special task was to lay stress in plain words and the frankest of expressions, on the more spiritual side of the religion of Israel, and to draw the attention of the nation in all its parts, whether king or nobles, or priests or people, away from only the external side of worship to its kernel, worship in the heart. Not the multitude of beasts trampling the Temple courts on their way to be sacrificed; not the outpouring of treasure; all these things together were of no significance in themselves, were of no permanent value in the sight of the LORD. Heart-service, heart-determination, mind and will wholly given up to Him—these are the things that matter; on these the prophets insist, and these are what they long for, and in vivid hope describe. This was the function of the prophets, this their privilege. Called of God, as the Jews ever believed, to peculiar fellowship with Himself, they were enabled to receive His communications, and to become more and more conscious of His own ethical holiness, and the high character of the demands which He made upon those who professed to serve Him.

Nor was this a late development in Israel's history. From the earliest days after the conquest of Palestine, persons arose (afterwards definitely called prophets) who endeavoured to see the moral reasons for secular troubles. *Israel hath sinned* was the summary of all their messages at such times, and repentance of sin the condition upon which amelioration was promised. The LORD was not only the Lord of the Hosts of Heaven; He was also the Captain-general of the armies of Israel; and secular victory depended upon ethical fitness to receive it.

Thus the idea of ethical holiness became more and more associated with the idea of God, and the necessity for such holiness was preached to His worshippers. This, and nothing short of this, became the main and leading subject of all the Old Testament writers, whether legislators, or historians, or prophets, or priests, or poets. Each in his own way, and in his own degree, taught that ethics were the supreme demand of the LORD, each insisted on the highest possible morality for those who would enter His courts; and each proclaimed His willingness to receive those who repented of their sins, and His ability to give to His people grace to exhibit a high ethical standard in their lives. This was the subject of all the Old Testament writers, this their hope, this their dream of dreams. Nothing less than this underlay all their rites, all their narratives, all their sermons, poems, and even apocalypses. This and nothing less, and there can be nothing more.

Further, it surely was very natural that such Old Testament saints, as they meditated on holy things, and, as they believed, had their meditations illumined by the Spirit of God, should expect that the perfect understanding of the will of God, together with the perfect ability to fulfil it, should be found first in one person, before such understanding and ability were passed on to the nation generally. In other words, it was only natural that the Old Testament writers should look forward to a Messiah.

John the Baptist then was in the true line of prophetic succession when he summoned men to repentance. Why was his cry rejected by the leaders of the nation?

Can the reason be that they were more interested in, shall I say, the intellectual side of religion than its spiritual claims? For religion has a strong intellectual side. Every student of his Bible knows this. He finds it intensely interesting to discover little by little this or that fact in Holy Scripture; he welcomes with keen enjoyment every fresh discovery, in the contents of cuneiform tablets, or on broken potsherds, which throws light upon its meaning. If his duty is to lecture, he enjoys telling his pupils all that he himself has learned; if he is a preacher, he bids his congregation admire afresh the accuracy of the Divine oracles. Or, again, he may have been convinced long ago that God gave His final message in sacred Writ, and that to him has been entrusted in late succession the privilege of learning to apply its orders to the changed circumstances of modern life—always, be it understood, in agreement with the lines of sound exposition How he loves to trace out the new, yet ever old, methods used by God in proclaiming the Truth! He gladly devotes his time and energy to unfolding the relation of the Law of God to the things of to-day.

Yet, student and teacher though he is, surely he is always conscious that increasing knowledge of these things is not identical with increase of spiritual life, and does not necessarily stand in close connection with it.

Can the reason why the rulers of the time rejected John the Baptist be that they lacked this spiritual perception? Can it be that they were satisfied with their own spiritual state, although he cried to them: *Repent?* Can it be that he might have said to them what the Christian mystic told some of his enquirers, that they were already as good as they wished to be?[1]

Many Christian readers of this book will be beginning to ask: Is not the book intended to be read by Jews, and must they not be shown in no uncertain language that one important part of the *raison d'être* of the Old Testament is to point them to the Messiah? No doubt this is so, but, I fear, hardly in the sense that those readers mean. For they imply that scattered throughout the Old Testament are definite predictions of the Coming, the Life, the Work and Death of the Messiah, and that these predictions have been fulfilled in Jesus of Nazareth.

This, no doubt, has been the opinion of almost all Christians, and has formed the greater part of the arguments adduced in the various treatises against the Jews which have been composed in almost every decade from the first century onwards. Of course difficulties have often been felt about such passages, and it has often been supposed, that, when an Old Testament writer was speaking of high ethical claims in general, he sometimes broke off his description of his hope in general to speak of the Messiah in particular, the previous statements being pictures of what the nation ought to be. If this were true, then indeed it would be necessary to decide in each case whether a passage referred to the Messiah as such or not. And it cannot be denied, that this opinion has been held by both Jews and Christians for centuries, and has lain at the root of thousands of controversial volumes. In fact, it has seemed so important that the controversialists on either side, Christian or Jewish, have spent most of their time in affirming or denying (with equal positiveness) the legitimate reference of these passages.

I do not propose to take part in any such controversy. And this for two reasons.

First, it becomes a merely intellectual warfare. Suppose the Jew does see the overwhelming truth of the Christian's arguments: what of that? Is he any nearer God? At most, one of the intellectual barriers has been broken through, and the intellect is only an outer rampart. The citadel is the will, the heart, the real desire for spiritual things. Very little indeed is accomplished until that is stormed and won. Faith in Christ is not like mastering a proposition in Euclid, which moves on in steady argument from premiss to proof, until at last the intellect is fully convinced that such and such is the result, and cannot be otherwise. Our Christian forefathers, we must confess, saw in the Old Testament a vivid and detailed life of Jesus of Nazareth, centuries before He lived on earth. They were astonished that Jews did not accept the picture thus drawn, and did not follow even the interpretation of the passages adduced. Yet even if they had succeeded in persuading the Jews of the accuracy of both interpretation and application, what would they have done? Jews "converted" in intellect alone would have been no nearer the Truth than before. They would not necessarily have become followers of

Jesus of Nazareth, for His cry like that of John the Baptist, was "Repent."

Secondly, and of even greater importance, is the very fact that there is really uncertainty about so many of these predictions. And this suggests the possibility that some are not predictions at all in the sense intended. The prophets may have been otherwise occupied than in drawing verbal pictures of the future, composing the outlines of the history of the Lord Jesus, or even the details of His life and death and ascension, and the outpouring of grace upon the Church. Such predictions have indeed been seen in the Old Testament by many great scholars, and have been keenly defended by some, and by others as keenly attacked And all the time the assumption of both Jews and Christians may well have been wrong, because unnecessary. May it not be that the Old Testament writer was so entranced with the subject of ethical claims, *i.e.* of holiness in our sense of the word, that he naturally, so to say, sometimes described them as exhibited in a person, without intending to make a prediction at all?

"What!" cries some Christian reader, "no predictions of my Saviour, the Lord Jesus, in the Old Testament! Where then is my faith on Him? Is it not destroyed?" No, my friend, for surely you do not believe on the Lord Jesus because of the Old Testament. You in reality believe on Him because of what you learn about Him in the New Testament, and then you turn back to the Old, and find your faith in Him confirmed.

"But," you say, "this book is partly for Jews, and your object is, professedly, to win Jews to Christ.

You ought, therefore, to bring to their notice some, at least, of the many predictions of Him in the Old Testament Were our forefathers indeed wrong when they set themselves to prove the Christian belief in Jesus of Nazareth from the verbal predictions contained in the Old Testament?"

To speak quite frankly, there is a better way, and the cause of Christ needs the better way only, and does not require to be supplemented by doubtful claims. For it may well be that it is of very little importance whether any particular passage in the Old Testament is a definite prediction of Christ or not. By "definite" I mean, defined in the conscious intention of the prophetic writer. For we are not in a position to say what was the definite intention of the Divine Author, and in what cases the Holy Spirit overruled the human amanuensis (if one dare use so strong a term) to write certain phrases. What really was, and is of importance, is not the conscious prediction on the part of the man, or even (speaking with reverence) the purposeful overruling on the part of God, but the deep sense of the moral demands of God Himself, the LORD of Hosts, upon mankind, and the glad vision of their being recognized and fulfilled.

Thus, it is of little consequence that the wording of some passage corresponds to an event, great or small, in the life of Jesus, but of the greatest importance that there should be a prophetic vision of those moral claims of God revealed by His prophets becoming an accomplished fact. That is not "prediction" in the common sense of the word, but the utterance of the prophet's faith, the outcome of his joyful expectation of the trustworthiness of the Divine promise; and of his glad hope of the blessed result of the full acceptance of His glorious and all-embracing Rule, those applied principles of God and His character, which in later times were called the Kingdom of Heaven.[2] But this must be accepted; and if people are satisfied with anything short of this, and reject it when it is set before them, they do so to their grievous loss.

I am not denying that there may be passages in which the writers of the Old Testament consciously referred to the Messiah. I think there are, and I will presently mention such passages; but what I want to insist upon is this: that even these passages must not take a prominent place in the evidence for the truth of Christianity.

There is no difficulty in understanding how the Church came to use the Old Testament so readily as a storehouse of such "proof-texts." The early Christian writers employed the Old Testament in precisely the same way as the Jews used it. No doubt the direct evidence for this use among Hebrew or Aramaic-speaking Jews is of rather later date than the first century. But Greek-writing Jews like Philo and Josephus practised that use, and there is every reason to suppose that they reproduced the common habit of their contemporary fellow-Jews in Palestine and elsewhere.

The method was this: to apply a passage in the Law, or, if necessary, in the other two less authoritative parts of the Old Testament, in such a way as to prove the validity of a "traditional" custom, or perhaps only to illustrate a homiletical lesson, while all the time the teacher who made the application knew perfectly well that this was not the original meaning of the word or verse. And his hearers knew this as well as he. But for him and them alike, the Scriptures were inspired by God, inspired, at least in the Law, down to every word and every letter, so that what could be read into a passage (perhaps even by the manipulation of the order of the letters) was meant by God to be taught by it.

The first Christians did but continue the practice to which they had been accustomed as Jews, and their successors followed their custom. Strictly speaking, needless to say, such applications of words and verses were not "proofs" in our sense of the term. And, no doubt many early writers were well aware of this. But it was forgotten, and the Church came to regard the passages as real proofs, however far-fetched and strained they appear to us to be.[3] Naturally there is no harm in drawing illustrations from Scripture, so long as they are regarded as illustrations only. For this is done daily by Christians and Jews alike, whether in private devotion or in public exhortation. But to give such illustrations the value of proof in the logical and almost legal meaning of the term, is to play fast and loose with our own common-sense, and to expect others to be as foolish as ourselves. We all now— at least the great majority of Christians and probably even of Jews—recognize that inspiration does not include the actual letters, or even necessarily the words as such.[4] God was pleased to guide men of very various natural powers, men with human feelings and human imperfections, to write the many portions of the Bible at many different times. And the Hebrew Bible never existed (so far as we know) as one whole in a text of precisely the same form in which each part was originally written. In any case, it has not pleased Him to bring even one part of it exactly as it was first composed, down to our own day.

I said that it is probable that certain passages in the Old Testament were composed with direct reference to the Messiah. And, although few scholars to-day would agree as to which these passages are, it is perhaps as well that some should be mentioned.

Among the most certain is Isaiah ix. 2–7 (1–6 Heb.), with, perhaps, the preceding verses viii. 19–ix. 1 (viii. 19–23). For, though the passage is in parts very difficult to understand, its meaning as a whole is plain. The prophet describes in glad hope the birth of Him who is to be the great Ruler, who will represent God (and perhaps more than "represent") in His reign of righteousness and ensuing peace.

We may also include Psalm lxxii, with its imagery of a world-wide Ruler of the highest ethical standard. Perhaps also we should add Psalm ii, though this takes incidents in David's life as the basis of its description of the future. Nor is it impossible that even Psalm xlv was always intended to refer more to the Messiah than to any ordinary king. And I, for one, would certainly include Psalm cx.[5]

But, frankly, as I have suggested before, what does it matter whether this or that passage was intended to speak expressly of the Messiah? The prophets and psalmists were so full of hope for the future, looking forward eagerly to the rule of God, with its insistence on the imperial claims and imperial power of the LORD, which was always and utterly pure and holy, that they were not concerned with the character and work of the Messiah alone, but with the whole glory of renewed men. They that do the LORD's will must, indeed, expect suffering at the hands of the ungodly—therefore one poet wrote Psalm xxii, with its expression of intense bodily and mental pain, and with its final burst of thanksgiving and praise.[6] Another psalmist insisted that, however good the sacrifices of beasts might be, yet the very fact that the LORD had hollowed him out ears showed that he must fulfil the LORD's will in a holy life (xl. 6).[7]

And this principle is surely the key to that great description of the willing and innocent Sufferer for the benefit of others, whose history is related in Isaiah lii. 13–liii. The question has often been asked whether the inspired author is painting the misery of the nation, present or future, or is sheerly and straightforwardly predicting the coming of the Messiah, who will suffer all these woes for the nation and others.

But if the above principle of interpretation of the Old Testament holds good, the decision in favour of one or other of these alternatives is of no great value. For, according to that principle, the prophet is but using the figure of an individual to describe the true kind of service—even to death, if need be—in order that by utter self-sacrifice others may be helped, and he himself, in spite of temporary anguish, ultimately gain eternal glory. It is not unnatural, therefore, that when the Chancellor of Queen Candace asked the humble deacon: *Of whom speaketh the prophet this?*

he received no direct answer, and yet *Philip opened his mouth, and beginning from this scripture, preached unto him Jesus* (Acts viii. 27–35).

The prophet, that is to say, is not thinking either of the Messiah as such, or of the nation as such. He is concerned only with the ideal fulfilment of the will of God. For he is sure that this can be accomplished only by complete forgetfulness of oneself, and of one's own success in life, if only God be served and one's neighbour benefited. That is the substance of the prophet's message, and is indeed the very marrow of the whole Old Testament.

Suffering in doing the will of God! Complete submission to His will! An intense desire to know that will! A deep sense of failure, alike in learning it, and in doing it when learned! All this, and nothing less, is what the revelation of God in the Hebrew Bible is intended to convey. This it is on which its writers, the writers of every part, Psalms, Prophets and the Law, insist, and proclaim with as loud a cry and as penetrating a voice as they can produce. With this object it was that they framed their highest poetry, to charm the unwilling ears, and to convince the dull intellect; with this aim they formed their collections of laws and rules for holy cult and family life; with this purpose they dwelt in longing meditation on the will of the LORD, not carried away by a Divine afflatus, as were the priestesses of Delphi and the semi-heathen Balaam, but with mind and heart opened to the Divine teaching, learning the will of God for daily life, whithersoever that will might lead.

It was the lack of this desire with which Jeremiah

charged the religious leaders of his day. They were busy about sacrifices and the proper rules under which they were to be conducted, but omitted moral and spiritual matters of deeper import (Jeremiah vi. 20; vii. 21–24; viii. 8 *sq.*).

So with John the Baptist. The leaders of his time were, in a way, good men, but were occupied more with the lesser than with the greater things of life. They were eager enough to find out quite the correct method of offering sacrifices, with the strictly right way to obey this or that detail of the Law, that they might carry it out in the most minute point. For they were not "hypocrites" in the modern sense of the word. But with that aim of theirs and that performance they were content. They failed to grasp the great central message of God's revelation, *viz.* to learn and to do His will in moral and spiritual things. Therefore, John the Baptist cried *Repent*—and, alas, they refused to listen, like their fathers before them.

Second Part.

JESUS OF NAZARETH.

Not by army, and not by strength, but by my Spirit, saith the LORD of Hosts (Zech. iv. 6).

Chapter IV.

THE RECORDS; THE MIRACLES.

AMONG those who were baptized by John was a young man of thirty years of age, Jesus of Nazareth, who took up the Baptist's message and made it His own: *Repent ye, for the Kingdom of Heaven is at hand* (Matt. iii. 2; iv. 17). To the language of this cry we will return later.[1]

But we must first think of the Lord Jesus Himself.

It may indeed be asked whether the records of Him are themselves trustworthy? Do the Gospels give us the real facts about Him or not?

Now I am not concerned with such details as come under the head of what specialists call Textual Criticism, the study of the exact text of the Gospels as deduced from a comparison of the various manuscripts, versions and quotations in the early Church Fathers. For the Textual (*i.e.* the "Lower") Criticism has not touched any essential element in the text of the Gospels, interesting though the study of it is.[2]

Nor indeed am I much concerned with the Higher Criticism of the Gospels, *i.e.* the subjective analysis of the sources of the three narratives according to St. Matthew, St. Mark and St. Luke. Practically all scholars are agreed to-day that Mark is the earliest of the three, and that it was used by the two authors of Matthew and Luke, who also used another source, "Q," and each added some material peculiar to himself. It is, indeed, possible that in these three Gospels the sayings of the Lord Jesus may in some few cases have become tinged with the later thoughts of the minds of the writers, but, after all that the Higher Criticism has had to say, the general view of Him which the three portray remains unaltered.

Now when we endeavour to understand and to interpret to others the records of the Life of Jesus, we Christians dare not so disbelieve in the continuance of the work of the Holy Spirit as to belittle the Christian scholarship of our time. To disregard His present work is irreverence to God, and unbelief in His word. For although the Bible nowhere claims to be written from God's mouth, yet Christians accept its inspiration, although the limit and extent, otherwise the nature, of "Inspiration" is not only disputed, as has already been said, but probably is only to be learned with more and more exactness as time goes on.

Further, the nature of the inspiration of the New Testament records, or indeed the question whether they are inspired at all, is of little or no matter for our present purpose. For I shall not draw any lesson from the New Testament which is dependent on inspiration. It is quite enough for my purpose that its records are generally trustworthy, for, even were it to be proved beyond all reasonable doubt that some detail in them is inaccurate, this would not invalidate my argument.

In these few pages it will not be possible to draw more than an outline of the picture of Jesus of Nazareth given to us in the New Testament. But, before attempting even that, there is one subject which must be mentioned, because undue stress has been too often laid upon it. It has been argued with much learning and no little assurance that the fact that Jesus performed miracles is in itself sufficient to prove His Deity, and in consequence, the full rightfulness of His claim to our implicit belief and obedience. But is this the case?

It is indeed quite certain that He did perform miracles. Even the Talmud acknowledges this.[3] Attempts have been made, it is true, to eliminate miracles from the life of Jesus, but they have been failures, and to-day it is granted on all sides that one may reduce the Gospel narratives all one can and there still remains a residuum which contains miracles.

Yes, you say, somewhat grudgingly, we suppose we must grant this, but surely it appears to be true even of St. Francis of Assisi. In the later lives of the saint there is an innumerable list of miracles, and even after most of these are eliminated by a comparison of the first life, yet, even there a few miracles are related of him, so that we must believe that he too performed miracles.

Now does not this suggest the real value of the connection of miracles with Jesus of Nazareth? It is this. The miracles of Jesus do not prove, and were never intended to prove, that He is God. They do prove that He was a remarkable person. And, further, on the analogy of other persons of whom miracles are creditably related, whether they be Christians or Jews, or even heathen, that He was a sincerely godly person.

They do not prove more. The purpose of miracles is admirably summed up in the words of the widow woman of Zarephath to Elijah, when he had restored her son to life: *Now I know that thou art a man of God, and that the word of the LORD in thy mouth is truth* (1 Kings xvii. 24).

Let us be quite clear then why it was that the evangelists found it worth while to record the fact that Jesus of Nazareth worked miracles. It was partly because they wished to show His kindness in performing them, and this particularly in view of the further fact that He did not perform them without any cost to Himself. But especially because they knew that miracles suggested to all who saw or heard of them that He must have been a Person very near to God, and therefore trustworthy, and worthy of all credit when He spoke of spiritual things.

Observe in this connexion that miracles are regarded throughout the New Testament as intended not for the stupid, or for the spiritually careless; and again, that they never intended so to overwhelm a man by their greatness in being portents as to compel belief in Jesus. To conceive of miracles as intended to have this soul-compelling force, this compulsory conviction of mind, is to misconceive utterly and wholly the nature of the message of the Lord Jesus. In no single example does He make evidence of truth so plain and clear that it cannot fail to convince.

And this, we must remember, gives us the key to understanding why He did not perform a miracle just because He was asked to do so. He would not come down from the Cross when He was jeeringly invited.

JESUS: HIS MIRACLES

He would not appear to unbelievers after His resurrection. In either case to have acted otherwise than He did would have stultified His whole life and ministry. The appeal of Jesus to us is always made on moral grounds, never on those of mere logic, in the sense that we are logically compelled to the conclusion that we must believe on Him.

Intellectual difficulties were not the reason why the Jewish leaders rejected the message of John the Baptist. Were they the reason why they rejected the same message on the lips of Jesus?

Chapter V.

JESUS: HIS LIFE IN GENERAL.

We now come to the very centre of this book, the basis of our Faith, namely the Life of the Lord Jesus. But how can I describe this? How can I here exhibit Him as He ought to be exhibited?

For, in fact, there is only one way of exhibiting to the world the character and power of Jesus, namely, in our own persons and our own life. For though it is well, and indeed necessary, to state what the records of Him contain, yet life alone answers to life, and life can be represented in any fulness by life only. No written treatise, no spoken discourse, can correspond to the energy, the nature, the character of life. This has been forgotten, not only by controversialists but by theologians, and the results have been disastrous for the Church in general, and particularly for its influence on unbelievers.

It will be understood that I am not now laying stress on our duty of trying to resemble the Saviour. I am for the moment only stating the fact. Duty or no duty, there is no other way of portraying Him properly, and indeed no other way was proposed by Jesus Himself. Life can be represented only by life— not by pen and ink, nor even by words, however cunningly and eloquently they may be put together.

Here, of course, we are up against a paradox. If

Jesus can be presented to others only by life, how is it possible that He should ever be presented? For none of us is, or can be, like Him. Nor, in one sense, was it ever intended that we should be. The individuality of a person, the man himself, at any moment from his birth to his death, depends upon the total effect of the thousand and one factors that make up his environment and his reaction to it. That is one of the glories of the faith of all Theists. Every believer in God knows that he is not a fortuitous concourse of atoms, which is to cease when "the vital spark" goes out, but, on the contrary, a personality always growing, always developing, with no sign in it of ceasing to be, merely because the bodily frame in which the personality has touch with matter is itself dissolved. All Theists know that God is the real centre of their being, and that for them to leave this earth is only to change the mode of their existence, not to destroy it.

Hence the one object of the Theist's life is to manifest God in such ways and methods as He is pleased to permit, or, in the magnificent language of the Shorter Catechism, "The chief end of man is to glorify God, and to enjoy Him for ever." That is life Eternal; that alone is life worth living. Yes, and that alone makes it possible for us in any way to show forth the life of Jesus.

Show forth the life of Jesus! How can we? We do not live in Palestine, nor amid the details of a petty half-civilized State, as He did. We cannot even carry on our outer garments the sacred fringe which the woman touched to her restoration, and every Jew still wears, carefully concealed. The peculiar circumstances of all Jesus' life are not, and cannot be, ours. Is it then possible for us to show His life when our circumstances are so different from His? Yes, it is possible, and, in fact, demanded of us Christians. For life is not dependent on any one kind of environment.

> "We ask what offering we may consecrate
> What humble offering share.
>
> To steel our souls against the lust of ease;
> To find our welfare in the general good;
> To hold together, merging all degrees
> In one wide brotherhood;—
>
> To teach that he who saves himself is lost;
> To bear in silence though our hearts may bleed;
> To spend ourselves, and never count the cost,
> For others' greater need."[1]

Life is living, and if Jesus were visibly present among us to-day He would use our present circumstances and our present conditions to live out His life. It is that life, Jesus' life, in that meaning of it, that we have to exhibit. And we can do so. We Christians believe in the Holy Spirit, and in the Holy Spirit as the Divine Demonstrator of His life, and as the enabling power for our own.

We do not need then, nor do we wish, God forbid, to copy Jesus in His clothes or His food, or His use of His temporary and peculiar circumstances. But we do desire to catch the tone of His life on earth, and to see how Christ would have lived to-day if He had been in our place. That is all—and it gives the true reply to the absurd suggestion that we should never refuse to give something to a beggar—because in His day that was the only method of helping him (Matt. v. 42) and that we should not wear two coats—because in His day this savoured of luxury (Mark vi. 9). And so on. Our aim as Christians is to present Jesus to others in His character as He was, and still is, without attempting to imitate His mere actions as such. To try to do so would only mean that we had completely misunderstood the intention of His words.

For, after all, it is very easy to under-estimate the extent to which the life of Jesus has already been exhibited in the lives and actions of His followers. The Jesuit Fathers, who preached the Glad Tidings to the Red Indians in Canada; the devoted Moravian missionaries, who for a hundred years or more were never absent from the lepers in Robbin Island; the members of the Church Missionary Society, who to-day are giving their lives to the largest missionary colony of lepers in the world at Purulia in Behar, treating them with the best science of our day, nursing them, and healing them in body and in spirit—these are but a few of the ways in which Christ's life is now to be seen. There are again the slum workers of Roman Catholic Sisterhoods and of the Salvation Army, and the untold efforts of Anglican clergy and their helpers. And there is in England the zeal for the education of the poor in school and university, begun and fostered by the clergy, until it grew so great that most of it has had to be handed over to the State. In all these and innumerable other ways the life of Jesus has been, and is being, lived out before our eyes. Let us praise God for it!

Would that we had always set this aim before ourselves, taking it as our standard from day to day, first as individuals and then as communities. But, alas, we have not done so. The true saints indeed of Christendom cannot be numbered for multitude, yet they are exceptions. The great majority of believers, even of true believers, have been content with a miserably low standard of spiritual life, ignorant of that to which they are called, and blind to the infinite possibilities within and without, upwards and around, which have been theirs to take. For the Church has been very backward, and even more so in its corporate capacity than in its individual membership. And as for political communities, even though many nations call themselves Christian, they have hardly pretended to try to exhibit Jesus of Nazareth. Nor indeed can we expect otherwise so long as the greater part of electors to Parliament, and of elected members, make no such endeavour in their own persons.

In any case the result is this: No nation has taken Jesus of Nazareth as its standard of life. And not even has any branch of the Church risen to its privileges and pretensions. One or two small bodies of Christians have almost done so, notably the Moravians. But the Church, as such, Orthodox, Roman, Anglican, Lutheran and Reformed in its many off-shoots, have done very little to exhibit Him, to placard Him, as it were, before men's eyes, so that even while they run on this world's business they may read His life and work.

It is not the aim of this chapter either to apportion or to weigh the injury done to the cause of Christ by the failure of Christians individually or corporately to exhibit Jesus of Nazareth to the Jews. The fact that there has been, and still is, failure of a terrible kind cannot be denied. The wonder is that, in spite of this, so many Jews have become enamoured of Jesus and have come over to follow His banner.

The life then of Jesus of Nazareth can be portrayed only in life, and in this we Christians have failed. Yet we have the records, and we must fall back on them. But I do not propose to put forward even a summary of their contents. Many "Lives" of Jesus have been written in the last fifty years, some bristling with antiquarian and rabbinical knowledge;[2] some written in modern English and adapted to the liking of those who love flowers in literature;[3] some with Jewish knowledge and prejudices;[4] some with painstaking and believing insight.[5] There is an abundance of such "Lives" to suit the taste of all readers. I do not attempt to add to their number.

CHAPTER VI.

THREE TRAITS IN THE LIFE OF JESUS OF NAZARETH.

ALTHOUGH I have neither the ability nor the desire to add to the many Lives of the Lord Jesus, it is necessary to point out certain traits in His character which especially attract us who live in the twentieth century.

In the first place He was a strong man, a man's man, to use the cant of to-day. There was nothing weak or feminine about Him. The "Gentle Jesus, meek and mild" is a myth of our childhood. I say nothing about His physique, which is of little importance, though apparently it was first-rate. But of His courage, of His independence, of His firmness, of everything that goes towards making the first claim upon our admiration, there is abundance. What He said He meant and did, regardless of objections from friends and opposition from foes.

So far from yielding, He did not hesitate to reject mistaken opinions even when they were prompted by love to Him. His own mother and His brethren could not move Him when He knew that He was in the right (Mark iii. 31; *Cf.* 21), His chief disciple would hold Him back, but was sternly rebuked (Mark viii. 33). And as for others! They might be the most learned, and the most respected in the whole land, but if they would hinder His works of kindness (Mark iii. 1–6;

cf. ii. 17), or blame His followers unjustly (Mark ii. 23-28; vii. 5-23), or accuse Him falsely of blasphemy against God (Mark ii. 6-10), or say that He was in league with Beelzebub (iii. 22-30), or try to pose Him with a practical and very ingenious dilemma, He penetrated their subtlety and worsted them (Mark xii. 13-17). For He feared no one, and He did not hesitate to brave the fury of the mercenary High Priests by expelling the traders from the Temple precincts, much as Nehemiah drove out the son of Joiada of old (Neh. xiii. 28). But in the case of Jesus there was no animosity. A symbolic whip of three or four rushes, picked up from the floor, together with the effect of His own personality, was enough to clear them all out headlong.[1] And when the "authority" for His action was questioned, He retorted by placing His opponents on a moral dilemma. "Why," said He, "did you reject John the Baptist?" And they were afraid to give an answer. For they feared the people too much to tell a lie, and they feared God too little to tell the truth (Mark xi. 27-33).

He knew His own position, and claimed allegiance. He called fishermen to leave their nets and follow Him, and they obeyed (Mark i. 16-20). He summoned one of Herod's agents who was collecting the octroi, and he came at His bidding (Mark ii. 13-17). He sent a message that He needed a *colt, whereon no man ever yet sat*, and it was at His service (Mark xi. 1-7), and He said not a word in dispraise when He was greeted with shouts of Hosanna (Mark xi. 8-10). He gave commands even to the forces of Nature, and they obeyed Him (Mark iv. 41). He walked even on the waves of the tempestuous lake, that He might train His followers in trustful service (Mark vi. 47-50). So, again, He spoke and unclean spirits left their victims (Mark i. 21-27).

In the same confidence would He teach, making His own opportunities in towns, synagogues, private houses, and by the lake-side, to few or many (Mark *passim*), in substance and methods best suited to the capacities of those He taught (Mark iv 33 *sq.*), claiming that men should obey Him whatever might happen, putting Himself and the good news He brought them on an equality (Mark viii. 35). And all the time— or at least (if you so insist) during the latter part of His ministry—He was expecting death at the hands of those He came to help, but He still went forward in His work fearlessly, and that with sure hope of ultimate triumph (Mark viii. 31; ix. 31; x. 34).

Yet, with all this, there is no trace of excitement or ecstasy; only the calm assurance that He was doing, and would bear, His Father's will (Mark xiv. 36). A strong life indeed, and singularly attractive. Who will catch the spirit of the life of Jesus, and try to follow Him?

While independence and firmness of character are the first visible and outward sign of greatness, there is an even stronger attraction in freedom from self-absorption. I know not what more positive phrase there is, for, though "accessibility" suggests part, it falls far short of the whole of what is meant. In any case, there is in Jesus of Nazareth the charm of never being in a hurry, though always occupied; of never being grieved for a moment at being interrupted in

His work, even though this might seem to be a matter of life and death. You remember the incident that I have specially in mind? Jairus, a ruler of the synagogue, had summoned Him in haste, for his little daughter of twelve years old, was dying. He obeyed the call, and on His way was stopped. By whom? By a poor woman who had been ill for twelve years—the similarity of time made the incident more easily remembered—who in superstitious reverence, yet with very real faith, touched the *Tsitsith* which hung on the corner of His robe. She was healed, He being fully conscious of His action in healing her, but, that so she might lose nothing of all that His healing might bring, for soul as well as for body, she was brought to confess publicly her need and her faith. But the delay cost time, and Jairus' daughter grew worse, and died. Had Jesus then made a mistake in His willingness to be interrupted? "My times are in Thy hands!" He might have said. For when we do what God sends us there can be no mistake. And *the little girl rose up and walked, . . . and He commanded that something should be given her to eat* (Mark v. 21–43).

Again, He was teaching, and little children came clambering up around Him. How could He go on speaking? He was being interrupted, and His disciples would fain push them away. But for Him to be "interrupted" made no difference; to an ideal servant of God "Disappointment is His appointment"; and He welcomed the children, taking them up in His arms and blessing them, and then, using them as a fresh text, He found in them the very summary of His whole message: "Become like little children."

For true religion is not a matter of learning or acquirements, but a sense of helplessness and of simple trustfulness in God (Mark x. 13–16).

Or again, one day, as He is walking along, a rich young man runs up and kneeling down asks Him what he must do to obtain eternal life, and even adds the epithet *Good* to his address to the Master. The Lord Jesus listens at once, probes the young man's ignorance of what "goodness" really means, and while recognizing the sincerity as far as it went, gives him a test which in his case was vital. Are you willing, He asks, to give up everything—power, position, wealth, that you may help others more than yourself, and walk in poverty with Me? An acid test indeed for that young man, and, alas, he failed (Mark x. 17–22).

So again, on His solemn march from Jericho to the final scenes at Jerusalem, the whole procession is delayed by the importunity of a blind beggar, Bartimaeus. But Jesus stands still, that He may attend to him, and the blind man follows, praising God for the restoration of his sight (Mark x. 46–52).

Need I mention the incident of the interruption at the meal in Bethany? As He was reclining at meat, with His feet stretched out behind Him as usual, a woman breaks over them her costly cruse of spikenard, brought from the far-distant Himalayas, filling the house with the perfume, and, as it were, anointing His body for the burial. To the godless it seemed a waste, and if He Himself had been asked He would no doubt have had the money spent on the poor instead. But she was doing the best she knew according to her light; and He was not so self-absorbed in His teaching as to hinder her action (Mark xiv. 3–9).

While independence and firmness of character are the first quality essential to winning others, and the second is the charm of entire freedom from that self-absorption which is in reality a mark of innate selfishness, the third and greatest is love in action. It is hardly necessary to say that it is this which has been the most effective of all motive powers in winning admiration for Jesus of Nazareth. Many examples of this love have been given already in the preceding pages, including the cases of healing by Him. And these, it must be remembered, always cost Him something. They were not the result of mere words. For, as He definitely says on one occasion, "virtue," *i e* energy, went out of Him (Luke viii. 46). But the cost made no difference; He had the opportunity of showing kindness, and He took it. No doubt He has been blamed for discriminating as much as He did. Why, for instance (it has been argued), do we never read of kindness done to a Pharisee? But how could He possibly heal a Pharisee if the Pharisee maintained his supercilious attitude towards Him? The whole *raison d'être* of His miracles lay in the moral receptiveness of those whom He cured. He could not, was not able to, heal where there was moral opposition (Mark vi. 5 *sqq*).

But His acts of kindness recorded in the Gospel of St. Mark are so many that even to enumerate them would almost be a recapitulation of the whole Gospel. The reader would do well to read the little book for himself, and make a written note of each miracle,

Throughout, Jesus works miracle after miracle, mostly miracles of healing With unblemished conscience, therefore, He can say: *If any man would be first, he shall be last of all, and minister of all* (Mark ix. 35). For He Himself came *not to be ministered unto, but to minister, and to give His life a ransom for many* (Mark x. 45). It was, therefore, only to be expected that He should urge His followers to forgive others, if they wished their Father in heaven to forgive their own trespasses (Mark xi. 25).

Independence and firmness of character; freedom from all self-absorption, love continually showing itself in acts of practical kindness, are united in Him to a degree, and in a perfection far surpassing those seen in any other person Can you, in fact, find any flaw at all in Him?

The reader will not have failed to notice that thus far almost all my examples have been taken from the Gospel according to St. Mark. I have so limited myself on purpose, chiefly because that is the oldest record we possess as it stands, being written between A.D. 60 and 70, *i.e* only some thirty or perhaps forty years after the Crucifixion. And it must also be remembered that it itself is composite, and that its author, traditionally St. Mark, used documents which were written still earlier. We can hardly be wrong if we place these in the early fifties, say some twenty years after our Lord's death. And what are twenty years? To any man of forty years of age they seem as nothing. He remembers what he did twenty years ago as though he did it yesterday.

If, however, I were to use the two other Synoptic

Gospels, Matthew and Luke, the result would be the same. For, though they each have their peculiar additions or modifications, they tell essentially the same story as Mark, and present the same picture of the Lord Jesus. I do not say that it would be wearisome to the reader if I were to recount any fresh illustrations of the perfection, and so the attractiveness of the Lord. But it is unnecessary for my purpose. The reader can easily procure those two Gospels. Let him do so and read them for himself.

Two incidents, however, in the life of Jesus of Nazareth demand special attention; for both form very important criteria of His work. The first was at the commencement of His ministry, and coloured the whole of it, nay, was of its very warp and woof.

For immediately after He had been baptized He had a strange experience It was suggested to Him that He should use the same methods for success that were adopted by all leaders in business and adventurous enterprise. First, let Him care for Himself. His own health and physical energy were of primary importance, and, as He undoubtedly had unusual powers, let Him satisfy His own needs first, by working a miracle to provide Himself with food. But that was not His way. To have done so would have been to over-rule providence, *i.e.* the care of His heavenly Father for all men's requirements. A man's life does not depend ultimately on bodily food, but on the expressed will of God. "Better die than tell a lie," said the Oxford saint of the nineteenth century to his class of boys. That too was the attitude of Jesus. Let my Father's will be carried out in the way that He chooses, and all will be well!

Yet, again, while putting God first it surely would be wise at once to engage the people in His favour. A display to them of His power could do no harm! A miracle for Himself He refused to work, but a portent showing that He stood in an unique relation to God might draw them all over to His side, and save endless confusion and error afterwards! After all, God had promised Him complete protection (Ps. xci 12) Let His safe descent from the pinnacle of the Temple in the sight of the crowd of worshippers lead them to accept Him!

But, once more, He would have none of it. Trust His Father He would; but test Him, as Israel did of old in the wilderness (Num. xiv. 22), He would not His early training brought to His mind the words· *Ye shall not tempt the LORD your God* (Deut. vi. 16).

And then a far more subtle case was put before Him! Why should He not adopt the methods of other leaders? Who ever heard of a secular ruler, a parliamentarian, or even a social reformer, being too strait-laced and particular about the means He used? And even if it was not to be expected that He would deviate from the strictest lines of honesty and truth, yet surely He might well use ordinary and upright means. There is nothing like organization: organize to the very details! Put your strength into argument: be known as the great logician! Devise this means and that means of improving things, of bettering class conditions, of reducing slavery and other examples of oppression. Politics, politics, what can there be like politics! Do they suggest a little savour of the Prince of this world? No matter! A slight tendency to obey his orders as seen in plain human life is nothing worth considering! Take it, and your success is assured! The people and rulers of Israel will rally round you! Messiah as reformer, yes, and as, at last, deliverer from Rome, will be acclaimed by all! What more is needed?

It is the old cry, but never the cry of Israel's legislator, prophets, or psalmists: For they were taught of God, and He says to His people: *My thoughts are not your thoughts* (Isa. lv. 8).

The thoughts and the ways of the world are always very plausible, and yet thoroughly unsound, if real, solid, vital and permanent, welfare is to be accomplished. John the Baptist would have none of them; nor would Jesus of Nazareth Do we begin to see a reason why John and Jesus were alike rejected?

The second incident of great importance in the life of Jesus which has not yet been mentioned is what is known as His Transfiguration. Strangely enough, many Christian writers have failed to grasp its significance, although each of the three Synoptists considered it too important to be omitted.

They tell us that the Lord Jesus took three of His disciples, the three in whom He met with special sympathy and spiritual intelligence, into a high mountain (apparently one of the slopes of Hermon), and there was transfigured before their eyes. Even *His garments became glistering, exceeding white* (Mark ix. 3). But that was not all, nor indeed was it the chief part of the incident. For then the three disciples,

Peter, James and John, saw also Elijah and Moses, *and they were talking with Jesus (ibid.* ver. 4). The third evangelist, St. Luke, tells us the subject of their conversation, *His decease which He was about to accomplish at Jerusalem* (Luke ix 31). Thus, Jesus Himself was transfigured; Moses and Elijah conversed with Him; and the subject of their conversation was His approaching death.

What does "transfiguration" suggest? Such freedom, I suppose, from stain of sin, such perfection in duty performed, such complete obedience, negative and positive, to the will of God, that it was now evident to the whole universe of watchers that Jesus was now ready to be admitted into the courts of heaven. If Enoch was translated without seeing death; if Elijah was caught up by a whirlwind into heaven; if there was something strange about the departure of even Moses (Deut. xxxiv. 5 *seq.*), was it not fitting that one so faultless as Jesus of Nazareth should go straight to that bliss reserved for all the saints? Angels may have supposed so; we know not. Men would certainly have thought so But Moses and Elijah, men who have been the media through whom the LORD had expressed His will in the Law and in prophecy, knew better, aware that to complete the full purpose of the Father, to fulfil the ideal of the Old Testament, He who would accomplish the will of God must obey it, even to death. Obedience is perfected only if it is carried out to the very utmost. Self-sacrifice, and nothing short of self-sacrifice, is the ideal of life, and, if others are to be benefited, is a necessary process in bringing life to them. If Jesus were not to

JESUS: THREE TRAITS IN HIS LIFE

pass through death, He would neither be a complete example, nor would He accomplish anything to which the portraiture of self-sacrifice in the Law and the Prophets pointed.

So we see Jesus; Jesus the strong man in His independence, courage and firmness, Jesus, free from self-absorption, accessible at all times to men, women and little children, to whoever wished to come near Him; Jesus, giving of His best, at His own cost, in His loving willingness to help, yet also Jesus, in complete obedience to His heavenly Father, trusting Him for His own needs, yet not presuming on unauthorised risks, and, above all, daring to follow heavenly methods alone, unsmirched by worldly tricks; and, once more, Jesus, willing to follow His Father's plan, to obey Him at all costs, even to death itself.

Who can claim our love as does Jesus?

CHAPTER VII.

THE KINGDOM OF HEAVEN.

Now that we have seen that Jesus of Nazareth fulfilled in His life on earth the prophets' expectation and vivid hope that the principles, the moral purposes, of God would be seen in practice, it is well to examine more closely what Jesus Himself said about the nature of those principles.

The Kingdom of Heaven is at hand. So cried John the Baptist; so also cried Jesus of Nazareth (Matt. iii. 2; iv. 17). What did they mean by the phrase, and how was the kingdom at hand? Now we dare not assume that the phrase *the Kingdom of Heaven* on the lips of John and the Lord Jesus meant precisely and solely what it meant on the lips of their audiences. For to do so were to limit the thoughts of great thinkers by those of small. But if John and the Lord Jesus were to be understood, their words must have conveyed something to the minds of those to whom they spoke. What then was the meaning already attached to the phrase?

Now it is not possible to prove here at any length what that meaning was It is enough to remind ourselves that in that phrase the word *Heaven* is a surrogate for *God*, and that *Kingdom* does not mean (as in English) a sphere over which God reigns, but the principles of His rule. A more exact translation in English would be The Rule of Heaven. Two quotations will suffice.

R. Jochanan (c. A.D. 250) said, "He that would accept the yoke of the kingdom of heaven in perfection, let him cleanse himself, and wash his hands and lay tephillin, and say the Shma', and say the Prayers, and this is the kingdom of heaven in perfection."[1]

As Dr. Schechter writes: "Communion with God by means of prayer through the removal of all intruding elements between man and his Maker, and through the implicit acceptance of God's unity as well as an unconditional surrender of mind and heart to his holy will, which the love of God expressed in the *Shema* implies, this is what is understood by the receiving of the kingdom of God."[2]

It would then be a mistake to suppose that on Jewish lips the phrase "the kingdom of heaven" referred only to the future. On the contrary, it expressly included the present. According to Jewish teaching it was the rule of God, and this was to be accepted heartily by individuals, and observed here on earth as far as it now can be, but to be accepted fully and obeyed perfectly, both in Israel and throughout the earth, only in that blessed time still future, when, by the direct action of God, the supreme King, all hindrances shall have been removed. In other words, the kingdom of heaven is the rule of God carried out in those principles of action which are characteristic of God, in daily practice here and now, though indeed it is only hereafter that they will be grasped and observed in their fulness, and their perfect application.

"God the supreme King." For almost without

exception in Jewish writers[3] the supreme King of the kingdom of heaven is not the Messiah, but God. And this is presupposed in many of the sayings of Jesus of Nazareth. One parable relates the Marriage of the Son of the King (Matt. xxii. 1–14). Again, He bids His disciples pray. *Our Father . . . Thy Kingdom come* (Matt. vi 9, *seq.*). Again, He says: *Your heavenly Father knoweth that ye have need of all these things; but seek ye first His kingdom and righteousness* (Matt. vi. 32, *seq.*). So, *the righteous shall shine forth as the sun in the kingdom of their Father* (Matt. xiii 43). And, again, the Lord Jesus says that He will drink new wine *in My Father's Kingdom* (Matt. xxvi. 29). He proclaimed God as the supreme King, in accordance with the prevailing Jewish opinion.

Again, the Lord Jesus exhibited in His own life the fulfilment of the rule of God, and this was the "coming" of the kingdom of heaven so far as this was possible in the case of one Person. But it is self-evident that, great and unique as this fulfilment of the hope of the prophets was, they contemplated the eventual issue as much more than even that. This further fulfilment was the chief object of the ministry of the Lord Jesus. He endeavoured to bring it about not only by what He was and did, but also by what He taught.

We must, therefore, briefly consider at least some of the chief principles of the rule of God on which He insisted.

The first and greatest of these principles is: *Blessed are the poor in spirit, for theirs is the kingdom of heaven* (Matt. v. 3). Perhaps the actual phrase used by Jesus was only *Blessed are ye poor*, without the addition of *in spirit* (Luke vi. 20), but poverty as such is neither bad nor good, and if that is the original form of the saying, Jesus will have used it only as a paradox, to call the attention of the careless. For not poverty in this world's goods, but conscious poverty in spirit (as St. Matthew expands the saying), is all-important, *viz.* the sense of unworthiness, the knowledge that one's merit is infinitesimal, the humility that made the publican in the parable be *unwilling to lift up so much as his eyes unto heaven*, so that *he kept smiting his breast, saying, O God, be merciful to me a sinner* (Luke xviii. 13).

This principle stands at the head of the whole Sermon on the Mount, and rightly so For it represents the crucial difference between the comparatively superficial religion of mere ecclesiastics and schoolmen, whether they be Jews or baptized Gentiles, and the real Christian teaching of the New Testament. The Lord's words are hateful to the "natural man," and are despised by the merely intellectual, and are considered insufficient by even the would-be conscientious. But they are the very core and centre of the teaching of Jesus: Down, down, before God, they cry aloud to us! Remember that you are sinners, and can do nothing of any weight to "deserve" pardon. But if you come before God as really poor, then the kingdom of heaven is yours.

This truth is reiterated by Jesus under different modes of expression. *The meek shall inherit the earth* (Matt. v. 5). To the disciples' enquiry, *Who then is greatest in the kingdom of heaven?* Jesus, for answer, encircled a little child with His arms, and set him in their midst, and told them that unless they became like such little children they would not enter into it. *Whosoever therefore shall humble himself as this little child, the same is the greatest in the kingdom of heaven* (Matt. xviii. 1–4). And, again, He tells them on another occasion that little children must be allowed to come near Him, *for the kingdom of heaven belongs to such as these* (Matt. xix. 14). Again, it is the publicans and harlots, who, on their repentance after their refusal to obey, precede the professedly religious into the kingdom of God. For when John the Baptist came, representing the demands of righteousness, the leaders of the nation refused to believe him; but the publicans and the harlots believed him, though the leaders did not even follow their example (Matt. xxi. 31–33) Not human merit, but sincere turning to God in deep humility of mind, ensures admission into the kingdom of heaven.

That is the first and great principle of the rule of heaven which the Lord Jesus taught His followers— deep humility of heart and mind and soul. The second is that the acceptance of that rule must have the fullest possible effect upon the daily life. For the Lord Jesus says: *Except your righteousness abounds even more than that of the Scribes and Pharisees ye shall not enter into the kingdom of heaven* (Matt. v. 20). Did He mean that, in spite of all the study given by devout students to the Law, its enactments could be divided up still more exactly; that the 613 commands might, with additional care and investigation, be found to number perhaps 620 or 630; that this or that traditional "hedge" against breaking one of those commandments, either by omission or by commission, might well be strengthened and multiplied? In a word, did He mean that, after all, improvements could be made in the meticulous study of various forms of good actions directed towards God or man? Was He really concerned, as were the leaders of the day, with externalities of cult or behaviour, presupposing (it must be remembered) that these were all performed quite conscientiously[4]? No, the principles of the rule of heaven are such that they must of necessity be effective in the lives of believers, if believers are to share in them. The servant who has been forgiven must forgive others, or he himself ceases to be forgiven (Matt. xviii. 21–35). This is no arbitrary fiat on the part of the servant's Master, but belongs to the very essence of the principles of the rule of God. That rule starts in the heart and will, and must, of sheer moral necessity, work itself outwards, to be seen at last in every detail of thought, word and act, affecting the whole life of the believer, in himself, in his relation to God and towards his neighbour.

For a self-centred religion cannot be in accordance with the character of God, who is nothing if not social. Therefore, it is that many of the demands of the Lord Jesus are connected with the exercise of our duties towards others. Those opponents of Christianity, or even its so-called friends, who assert that Christianity is chiefly occupied with saving one's own soul, are under a delusion. On the contrary, it bids us, just because we are followers of Jesus of Nazareth, do our utmost for others, bodily, mentally and spiritually, whether they are, like ourselves, believers in Him, or unbelievers. We dare not be cheese-paring in our care for others, we dare not limit it to those who are professedly of the same faith as we are. And if to love the whole world, and consciously serve it, be too vague an object, beyond our grasp, there are at least the ever-widening circles of family, parish, county, state, all of which have a very close claim upon us, and none is beyond our thought and energy.

Through all these spheres the kingdom of heaven, the rule of God, must spread, and every believer must take his share of spreading it so far as he is able to assimilate its meaning, and has opportunity of action. No sphere can be exempt. Even Hegel said that the State is, in its ideal, "the footstep of God in the world,"[5] *i.e.* to be marked with the principles of the kingdom of heaven.

The expression of the principles of the kingdom of heaven by individual believers is so important that the question at once arises whether these believers form a definite society, sharply marked off. Now individuals who are in personal union with God must *ipso facto* be in union with one another. To be sons of God implies family relationship. They must form, they cannot help forming, a society of the closest possible nature, *a body, supplied and knit together through the joints and bands, increasing with the increase of God* (Col. ii. 19).

And more than that. For this might in itself be true of a body that was solely and purely invisible. But such a conception cannot apply in all respects to a society of men and women upon earth who are joined in spiritual relationship. It is impossible that the spiritual life should not show itself in external actions, and that persons performing these should not become in some measure marked out from others, known and identified to themselves and all men by the practices they pursue. Believers as such cannot help becoming a society distinguished from others, whether these be individuals or groups.

Yet there is not a hint in the Synoptic Gospels that if it were possible for a believer in Christ to be outside that visible society he would necessarily be outside the kingdom of heaven. The kingdom is never identified with the Church. In the parable of the Tares, the field is expressly defined not as the Church but as the world (Matt. xiii. 38). And when the Lord Jesus tells Peter that upon him He will build His Church, He also adds that He will give him the keys of the kingdom of heaven (Matt xvi. 18 *seq*). For Peter was the first to express his faith in Jesus as the Messiah, so that on him all other believers have been built up, and again, he was the first to learn the great principles of the kingdom, and his interpretations of them still hold good.[6]

While then the highest claims are made in the teaching of the Lord Jesus, as recorded in the Synoptic Gospels, for the kingdom of heaven, and for absolute submission to it, the kingdom is not identified with the visible body of believers which we call the Church. For the kingdom of heaven is not a realm at all, much less a certain body of believers of which any human beings are the visible rulers. It is not the realm, but the rule of God.

The recognition or non-recognition of this affects our

whole attitude to current thought, social and political.[7] If government, as such, is first laid down for us Christians, and then righteousness, in the widest and fullest meaning of the word, is to be the result of good government, we shall perforce mould our ideas in conformity with that government. Whereas, if the principles of the kingdom of heaven are to be the norm of our lives, then the government of the State, or of any combination of States, will receive the final impress of moral excellence in the distant future only. The former theory was accepted all through the Middle Ages, and, confessedly, the result as seen in society and politics was very poor. The latter may well have its chance now and henceforward, with the result, as I believe, that the principles of the kingdom of heaven, of the sovereignty and rule of God, will at last run in all our lives and institutions, secular as well as Divine.[8]

Observe what this means—nothing less than that personal union of believers with Christ, as they yield themselves in ever-increasing degree to His will and purpose, will be worked out in truth, in morals, in righteousness, in love, affecting not the individuals alone, but the whole community and nation in which they dwell. "There is no distinction between the individual and corporate good. Man's deepest interest is union with his fellow-man. 'There is nothing,' said Spinoza, 'more useful to man than man.'"[9] Indeed, "the better a man understands his world, the more clearly will he see the social reactions of any of his decisions, the finer will be his own life, and therefore the kind of service that he renders to his world, and the more worthy he will find his world, both of his understanding, and of his service."[10]

There is, however, one condition of success in furthering the kingdom of heaven which is often overlooked—the condition that the acceptance of the rule of God includes whatever such acceptance may involve. And that may mean, and probably always does mean, suffering of one kind or another, and of less or greater degree, physical or mental. *He that doth not take his cross and follow after Me, is not worthy of Me*, says the Lord Jesus (Matt. x. 38). And again, *If any man would come after Me, let him deny himself, and take up his cross, and follow Me* (Matt. xvi 24).

No one likes suffering; it is the very essence of suffering that it should be unpleasant; yet it may be borne with fair ease if the sufferer recognizes that by his suffering others are benefited, perhaps even in their temporal, but certainly in their spiritual good. Shelley, it will be remembered, boasted of his atheism, and yet in his *Prometheus Unbound* he might almost have been describing the Lord Jesus of Nazareth. And his poem ends thus:

> "To suffer woes which Hope thinks infinite,
> To forgive wrongs darker than death or night;
> To defy Power, which seems omnipotent;
> To love, and bear; to hope till Hope creates
> From its own wreck the things it contemplates;
> Neither to change, nor falter, nor repent;
> This, like thy glory, Titan, is to be
> Good, great and joyous, beautiful and free;
> This is alone Life, Joy, Empire and Victory."[11]

For, in spite of the poet's pretensions to atheism, Christian truth had gripped him so firmly, that in describing the sorrows and endurance of Prometheus, he could not but portray also the fundamental truth of all true religion, that the Cross is the means by which the kingdom of heaven comes for all men; that the Cross, the Cross alone, for us in our measure, for the Lord Jesus without measure, is the one means of saving others, of bringing them to perfection of body and of soul. Self-sacrifice, the Lord Jesus would teach us, is necessary for all successful work in the kingdom of heaven.

Away with everything else for the sake of the kingdom of heaven! Yes, we ought to be willing that all we have should go, if only we were permitted to spread its principles! It is for this reason that the Lord Jesus could tell His disciples that there are persons who, like Jeremiah (Jer. xvi. 2), deny themselves married life *because of the Kingdom of Heaven* (Matt. xix. 12).

"If it be true," writes a modern philosopher, "that life comes only from life, then life must be sacrificed in order to produce fresh life."[12] Can we then be surprised that the Lord Jesus, with His more than Socratic method of going to the very root and spring of things, should proclaim the Cross as the one great means of human progress, and put His own teaching into practice? Blood and iron may, no doubt, found an empire; but they cannot maintain it. "It was no accident that Christianity is the religion of the Crucified. The Cross is but the culminating expression of a spirit which was characteristic of it throughout. An idea like that of Islam, making its way by the sword was abhorrent to it from the first. Its peculiar note is victory through suffering."[13]

Surely, as we study the teaching of the Lord Jesus, our hearts are moved, our cravings after complete surrender to the will and work of God are deepened, and our eyes are given keener vision of all that is involved in the acceptance of "the yoke of the kingdom of heaven."

Yes, I can imagine a reader saying, it is all very beautiful, but very unpractical in this work-a-day world. Many of the laws of the kingdom as Jesus of Nazareth Himself enunciates them are quite impossible to be observed, especially in the present state of society and civilization. If the laws laid down on the Sermon on the Mount were carried out, civilization as we know it would perish.

That in itself may be disputed, but I do not care to raise the discussion. For a false premiss underlies the objection, namely that the sayings in the Sermon on the Mount were ever intended to be "laws" in the usual connotation of the word. After all, you must credit the Lord Jesus with some common-sense. Surely He knew as well as anybody that it is impossible to satisfy the demands of every beggar, though He does say, *Give to him that asketh thee* (Matt. v. 42) [14] Surely He was not quite so foolish as to forget that if thieves and highway robbers are to steal and injure with impunity, social order will come to an end; and yet He says: *Resist not him that is evil: but whosoever smiteth thee on thy right cheek, turn to him the other also*

(Matt. v. 39) And *Judge not, that ye be not judged* (Matt. vii. 1). But then you say, Why does He lay down these laws? He does not. He gave us also credit for having common-sense, and for wishing to penetrate into His true meaning. For nowhere does He lay down a single law which answers to the common notion of a law in jurisprudence. It is of great principles that He is speaking, principles which indeed are fundamentally true, but differ in their application with every single case. The real question is not whether He expects us to obey His words blindly and unintelligently, regardless of consequences, but whether we accept with the fullest readiness and willing joy the principles, and try to carry them out in conscientious regard for the real benefit of others, as we believe He Himself could have done.

That is why He came, to carry out the will of His Father, in its highest and deepest moral sense, to fulfil (that is to say) the kingdom of heaven; and it was this desire and this method which He endeavoured to teach His followers. Can you imagine a higher, and a more attractive, purpose in life than this—to spread by life and self-sacrifice the rule of God, the principles of the kingdom of heaven?

Chapter VIII.

THE FOURTH GOSPEL: THE CONSIDERED FAITH OF CHRISTIANS.

WE have seen Jesus of Nazareth in the completeness of His fulfilment of the rule of heaven, with all that this meant of utter devotion and self-sacrifice; Jesus in His independence, His freedom from self-absorption; and His practical love in every case of need. And our hearts have been drawn towards Him, saying of Him as the Shulamite of her Prince: *Yea, He is altogether lovely.* With her we cannot but add, *This is my Beloved, and this is my Friend, O daughters of Jerusalem* (Cant. v. 16).

We have seen also that Jesus of Nazareth not only lived out the rule of heaven for Himself, but also trained His followers in what it really meant, teaching them with all the prophets, that it was something far deeper than the fulfilment of rules for daily life and for worship, however conscientiously these were performed. The acceptance of the kingdom of heaven meant for Jesus of Nazareth the devotion of the whole man to God, affecting all his relation to men of every degree and state. A noble truth, put forward nobly by the Lord Jesus. For never man spake as He spake, or so acted up to His own words.

This is the beginning of the Christian Faith, its necessary foundation, apart from which the rest of the building falls.

But my readers have a right to expect more than this. For it is possible for this to be accepted, and, notwithstanding, for the legitimate consequences of that acceptance to be disregarded

To this further statement we must now turn.

It will have been noticed that thus far the information about Jesus of Nazareth and His teaching has been taken exclusively from the three Synoptic Evangelists. The reason for this limitation is that they represent facts about Him and His teaching which few persons of critical minds will dispute to-day. The narratives in which they are recorded are simple and straightforward This is not to say that there is no bias in them. Of course there is bias. All history is biassed in one direction or another. Mere annals are drier than dust, and hardly give any information when read. But let a historian take them, showing how this or that fact fits in; how they explain incidents or phrases recorded elsewhere; how, in a word, they are part and parcel of a whole scheme of the life of some person or some nation, and the annals spring into energy, fired with the passion and enthusiasm of the new writer. Not one of the three Synoptic Gospels is free from bias of this kind.

But in the case of the Fourth Gospel the tendency of the historian is plainer than in the Three. Its authorship indeed is of comparatively little importance For in any case it represents a deliberate attempt to give a deeper, fuller, and therefore truer, account of the Lord Jesus than the earlier Evangelists. The author of it knew their writings, and knew also that he was able to supplement these in many ways, and he felt it well that he should do so, for mistakes had arisen from the use of them alone.

Whether he was actually the Apostle St John is also of comparatively little importance The present writer thinks that he was, and that the arguments adduced to the contrary are insufficient to prove their case.

Further, if the author of the Fourth Gospel was indeed John the son of Zebedee, and also the disciple who leaned on Jesus' breast at Supper, whom Jesus loved (John xiii. 23; xxi. 7, 20), he certainly had unique opportunities of knowing his Master's mind, and grasping the meaning of His life and words. He also had a long time to think over these, for, if he wrote about A D. 90, he must have been nearly eighty years of age.[1]

Naturally it is not possible to give a full account of the contents of the Fourth Gospel in one short chapter, much less to discuss it in detail; but as it stands for the considered Faith of Christians near the end of the first century of our era, a Faith which since that time at least (and, as I believe, for many years earlier) has been an integral part of Christianity, it is necessary to say something.

But one part, and that an important part, of its contents, I shall put on one side. I mean its history of the development of the conflict between the Lord Jesus and the leaders of the Jews That indeed is of thrilling interest, and perhaps ought to be included in this volume; but I propose confining myself to the Faith proper, the doctrine, as it may be called, of the Fourth Gospel.

It begins with a Prologue which enshrines most of the truths on which the Gospel insists. *In the Beginning was the Word, and the Word was in active relation to God, and the Word was God.* The author loses no time in stating that the Lord Jesus was God. For, shocking as the statement sounds to Jews, and shocking though the suggestion must have seemed to every enquiring Jew from the very first, the body of believers in the Lord Jesus had come to this conviction long before the time when the Fourth Gospel was composed. The author makes no more attempt to prove his statement than does the author of the Book of Genesis to prove his: *In the Beginning God created,* etc. In fact, as every one notices, the two statements are curiously alike in form.

In this resemblance, as all learned Jews know, there may be more than meets the casual eye. For Jews have ever found in the Hebrew term for *In the Beginning* (Brêshîth) more than an indication of Time or Pre-time. *Rêshîth* can mean so much. "For the sake of the Principal Thing"; "for the sake of" (or, if you will, "by means of") the Law; and even, if Messiah be regarded as the aim and head of God's revelation to man, "For the sake of," or, "By means of," or, "With the concurrence of, the Messiah."

Indeed, it may well be the case that the author of the Fourth Gospel had something like these midrashic expositions in his mind, when he starts off with *In the Beginning*.[2] Still, he does not choose any of them, but, like the author of Genesis, is really speaking of Time or Pre-time.

The Word. The term was common enough among

Jews. The Alexandrians, *e.g.* Philo, said "the Logos"; the Palestinians, "Memra." Both used it with as strong a personification as the author of the Book of Proverbs (viii. 22–31) used "Wisdom." But neither went beyond personification, or intended to suggest a separate personality.[3]

The author of the Fourth Gospel does. For him the Word is God, and yet is not identical with God, but stands in active relation to Him. Later in the Prologue he expressly identifies the Word with the Lord Jesus (*vv.* 14–18)

He thus deliberately accepts the full Godhead of Jesus of Nazareth, and states that that Godhead was before all time, and took human *flesh*, *i.e.* human nature in its entirety. Into subtle questions of the relation of personality and nature he does not enter. For he is not writing as metaphysician or philosopher, but merely states what he believes the facts to be.

The reader, however, may well ask, How was it that this stupendous faith in the full Deity of the Lord Jesus came about? How was it, he wants to know, that Jesus of Nazareth was believed to be God in the truest and fullest sense of the term?

One is disposed to answer that it was the result of careful investigation into our Lord's life, His perfection of character, His miracles, and so on. There is a great deal to be said for this reply, especially if one adds that Jesus seems to have Himself said that He was God, and that as He was eminently truthful and the very reverse of emotional and ecstatic, this claim of His must be accepted as true. No doubt the author of the Fourth Gospel saw the importance of such a mode of reasoning. For, in any case, it may be clearly deduced from his description of his Master.

Yet he himself adds another and more direct reason. He tells us that it was the conviction that the Lord Jesus had risen from the dead which produced this faith in His Deity. Thomas, a disciple already mentioned as a rather despondent but faithful person (xi. 16), of a cautious and enquiring mind (xiv. 5), steadily refused to believe in His resurrection. But when he had actual sight of Him, and had been even offered the opportunity of feeling His pierced side, he was wholly convinced, and addresses Him as *My Lord and my God* (John xx. 28). The resurrection of Jesus, in accordance with His promise (Mark ix. 31), convinced His followers that He was God (*cf.* Rom. i. 4). They were not concerned with the question how this was compatible with the great and supreme doctrine, supreme for Jews and Christians alike, of the Unity of God. They themselves knew with moral certainty that the Lord Jesus was, in spite of everything, very God, and they left the solution of the paradox to other ages.[4]

If, however, the author of the Fourth Gospel insists on the full Deity of the Lord Jesus, he no less insists on His Humanity. It was needful that he should. For then, as now, there was no little danger that believers should lay so much stress on the Deity of Jesus as to minimize His Manhood. Jews never seem able to understand this. They are for ever saying: If Jesus was God, how could He be tired when He sat by the well-side, or when He lay on the boatman's cushion, or be in agony in Gethsemane, and on the

Cross? They are even ignorant enough to speak of Him as "half-God and half-Man " But such terms only show their misunderstanding of what Christian teaching is. Christians believe, and their belief is brought out more clearly in this Fourth Gospel than anywhere else in the New Testament, that Jesus was wholly and altogether God, and was also wholly and altogether Man.

If Jesus was wholly Man, of course He could be tired, and be in bodily pain and mental agony. We know very little of the inter-relation of His Godhead and His Manhood, but being Man He must have been liable to physical weakness. Otherwise He would not have been Man in the ordinary and fullest meaning of the word.

That is our belief, and there is no use in opponents setting up a scarecrow—some figment of imagination— and throwing stones at it, instead of trying to understand what we do believe and why we believe it. Jews are ready enough to blame us for misunderstanding them and their religion; we ask for the same treatment from them which they ask of us.

A third subject in this Gospel should be mentioned because it gives the key to much in the life of Jesus. I mean the fact of His intimate communion with His Father in heaven.[5] This (like all else of primary importance) is mentioned in the three Synoptic Gospels also,[6] but not so fully or so plainly as in the fourth. The way in which it is made known to us in the Fourth Gospel seems strange at first. For the usual word for "pray" (*proseuchomai*), common in the three, occurs nowhere in the fourth. Did the author avoid it on purpose, lest his readers should suppose that prayer was a special and occasional thing with the Lord Jesus? In any case, while our author lays no stress on Jesus offering any formal prayers, yet the impression which the reader of his Gospel receives, and this from every page, is that the Lord Jesus was not in occasional, but in continuous, communion with His Father. With the Synoptics the Transfiguration was a single event; with the Fourth Gospel the whole life, all day and every day, was transmitting the Divine, because He never lost touch with it. The whole atmosphere of the Lord Jesus' life recorded in the Fourth Gospel breathes of God. Yet there is no indication of deification of His human nature. On the contrary, no Gospel lays so much stress on His humanity as this. But the perfectly Human is permeated through and through with the Divine.

Two of the Synoptic Gospels, it is true, give us a hint of this continuous fellowship in the words: *I thank Thee, O Father, Lord of heaven and earth, that Thou didst hide these things from the wise and understanding, and didst reveal them unto babes: yea, Father, for so it was well-pleasing in Thy sight. All things have been delivered unto Me of My Father: and no one knoweth the Son, save the Father; neither doth any know the Father, save the Son, and he to whomsoever the Son willeth to reveal Him* (Matt. xi. 25–27; *cf.* Luke x. 21, 22). And there follows in Matthew the glorious invitation to every needy soul: *Come unto Me, all ye that labour and are heavy laden, and I will give you rest. Take My yoke upon you, and learn of Me, for I am meek and lowly in heart: and ye shall find rest unto your souls. For My yoke is easy, and My burden is light* (xi. 28–30).

But in the Fourth Gospel the Deity of the Lord Jesus cannot be overlooked, much less can it be excised. The author is quite convinced of the full Godhead of the Lord Jesus, and he writes, as he says: *That ye may believe that Jesus is the Christ, the Son of God; and that believing ye may have life in His name* (xx. 31).[7]

It would be unjust to the author of the Fourth Gospel to mention only his description of the Lord Jesus Himself. For an integral part of the treatise is His relation to believers of all time. Hence the author is concerned with Him whom the Lord Jesus was to send from heaven to represent Himself on earth, and also with the maintenance of continued spiritual energy in His followers.

The first of these is the doctrine of the Holy Spirit. It is not my intention to discuss this polemically, but to state very briefly what believers in the end of the first century of our era held to be the truth. Probably the majority would have been very uncertain—to say the least—about His relation to the Father and the Son, for the orthodox belief in the Trinity was not yet precisely formulated.

Be that as it may, if the statements in the latter part of the Gospel were not so definite, we should be justified in understanding those references to the Spirit which are to be found in the earlier chapters as indicating only that rather vague notion of the Holy Spirit of God which we find in the Old Testament. But in the light of the later utterances the earlier are fairly certain. There is little doubt that when the author tells us that John the Baptist said he saw *the Spirit descending like a dove out of heaven* (i. 32), he had in his mind something more than a mere influence. The author almost certainly means that He of whom he will afterwards speak more clearly came down in special power upon the Lord Jesus at His baptism, thus enabling Him in His human nature to accomplish all He came to do, as, for example, to speak the message taught Him by God (iii. 34). For His words are in fact Spirit and Life (vi. 63).

So, again, a man's conversion is spoken of as the work of the Spirit, the result of the effect of the Holy Spirit of God upon him (iii. 8). Indeed, one of the Lord's comparatively early sayings is expressly explained by the author as referring to the definite promises of the later days (vii. 39).

These definite promises were given shortly before His death. For He would send One to His followers who should represent Him. *I will ask the Father, and He shall give you another Advocate, that He may be with you for ever, even the Spirit of truth. . . . He abideth with you, and shall be in you* (xiv. 16 seq.). *The Advocate, even the Holy Spirit, whom the Father will send in My name, He shall teach you all things, and bring to your remembrance all that I said unto you* (*ibid.* ver. 26). *When the Advocate is come, whom I will send unto you from the Father, even the Spirit of truth, which goeth forth from the Father, He shall bear witness of Me* (xv. 26). *When He, the Spirit of truth, is come, He shall guide you into all the truth. . . . He shall glorify Me: for He shall take of Mine, and shall declare it unto you* (xvi.

13, *seq.*). For He Himself, adds the Lord Jesus, will have left them, though He will be still alive· *I came out from the Father, and am come into the world: again, I leave the world, and go unto the Father* (xvi. 28).

So we come to the last point in the Fourth Gospel to which I wish to draw your attention. The author insists in every chapter that the Lord Jesus from the first (i. 4), and during His life on earth, and since His return to His Father, has been, and is, and will be, the one source of Life for this world, and, in particular, for those who believe on Him. What a majestic subject the author has! The Son has ever been the agent through whom the Father spreads Life. *As the Father has life in Himself so He gave to the Son to have life in Himself* (v. 26). *As the living Father sent Me, and I live because of the Father, so he that eateth Me— even he shall live because of Me* (vi. 57). *I am the Resurrection and the Life* (xi. 25). *I am the Way and the Truth and the Life* (xiv. 6). *For God so loved the world that He gave His only begotten Son, that whosoever believeth on Him should not perish, but have eternal life* (iii. 16). *He that believeth on the Son hath eternal life* (iii. 36). *Verily, verily, I say unto you, He that heareth My word, and believeth Him that sent Me, hath eternal life, and cometh not unto judgment, but has passed out of death into life* (v. 24). *He that believeth hath eternal life* (vi. 47). For, as Jesus says, *I came that they may have life, and may have it abundantly* (x. 10). *I give,* He adds, *unto them* (My sheep) *eternal life, and they shall never perish, and no one shall snatch them out of My hand* (x. 28).

There is also that long metaphor of partaking of

Him as Bread in Ch. vi. Many commentators, it may be noted, have supposed that the author is but expounding the doctrine of the Last Supper, but his object is much deeper than that alone. He wishes believers to understand that they must feed on Jesus, the Life-giver, as really—and indeed more really, if the spiritual is greater than the material—as one feeds on bread. So the Lord Jesus says of Himself: *My Father giveth you the true bread out of heaven. For the bread of God is that which cometh down out of heaven, and giveth life to the world. . . . I am the bread of Life: he that cometh unto Me shall never hunger, and he that believeth on Me shall never thirst* (vi. 32–35).

And, again, *I am the living bread which came down out of heaven: if any man eat of this bread, he shall live for ever* (vi. 51). So, slightly changing the metaphor, He says: *He that eateth My flesh and drinketh My blood hath eternal life; and I will raise him up at the last day. For My flesh is meat indeed, and My blood is drink indeed. He that eateth My flesh and drinketh My blood abideth in Me, and I live in him. As the living Father sent Me, and I live because of the Father; so he that eateth Me, he also shall live because of Me. This is the Bread which came down out of heaven: not as the fathers did eat, and died: he that eateth this bread shall live for ever* (vi. 54–58). *Because I live, ye shall live also* (xiv. 19).

Once more, that is to say, does the author of the Fourth Gospel bring out the surpassing value of the good news. We are not to be left alone, even though our Lord Jesus is no longer seen of mortal eyes. He died on the Cross indeed, but He lives, with, if anything, a fuller and more active life than ever. He is still near, working, apparently, by means of the Holy Spirit, and yet so intimate is the relation between the Spirit and the Son that the humblest believer, who allows himself to be led by the Spirit, has the privilege of such close communion with the Son as can be compared to nothing less than the assimilation of material food by the body. Partake of Christ, says our author; partake of Him; feed on Him; and so enjoy spiritual life to the utmost.

That is the privilege of the believer; to this feast we invite every reader.

Such was Jesus of Nazareth, and such His message according to the four Gospels. Yet He was rejected! Why? The reason is plain in the case of Pilate. Jesus demanded too much. Pilate failed to obey the claims of ordinary morality. The Roman governor had no use for justice if it conflicted with his own success.

And with Herod Antipas, the semi-Jew, the case is not otherwise. "Just a little miracle," said the Emperor to Savonarola. And Herod had so low a conception of what miracles meant that he hoped to see one wrought by Jesus. He put Him indeed on a level with the Baptist, and even went so far as to think John had returned from the dead. But he did not want to learn his duty to God from Jesus any more than from John.

But what of the leaders of the Jews? Why would they have none of Him? Why did they reject Him? Why did they reject John the Baptist? Why? There was one and the same reason—absence of any intense desire to know what was really right and to practise it—for it meant heart-felt humility before God, and utter self-sacrifice for men. The reason, that is to say, was not intellectual; it was psychological and ethical. They were too self-satisfied to become like the publican in the parable, and say, *God, be merciful to me a sinner* (Luke xviii. 13) Christ demanded of them something deeper, far deeper, than ordinary, though sincere, religion; and this they were so little prepared to give that they rejected His message—the same message as that of John the Baptist—and they brought Him to His death.

CHAPTER IX.

THE ATTRACTION OF THE LORD JESUS CHRIST FOR A BELIEVER TO-DAY.[1]

[So far I have written from the standpoint of a believer in Jesus of Nazareth as the Christ and the Very and Eternal God, and yet I have adduced only such arguments as may appeal primarily to a thoughtful and sincerely religious Jew.

But the reader will also like to know how such a belief in the Lord Jesus—with its implications—appeals to a Christian to-day. For in this way only will he arrive at a full understanding of our Faith. How is it that our Lord Jesus attracts us so much?]

"Our message is Jesus Christ. He is the revelation of what God is, and of what man through Him may become. . . . The Gospel is the answer to the world's greatest need. It is not our discovery or achievement; it rests on what we recognize as an act of God. It is first and foremost Good News. It announces glorious Truth. . . . We believe that men are made for Christ, and cannot really live apart from Him. . . . Herein lies the Christian motive; it is simple. We cannot live without Christ, and we cannot bear to think of men living without Him."[2] The words contain a fair estimate of the firm conviction of sincere followers of Jesus Christ throughout the world. We believe that the Gospel is in sober fact the answer to the world's deepest need, that in Jesus Christ of Nazareth men may find their every satisfaction; and we desire that all who read may feel the spell of the attraction laid upon us as we mark with spiritual understanding the beauty of the Christ.

We make no apology for our theme. We are aware that the Figure of Christ Jesus is the mark of the attention of mankind to-day to a degree perhaps as was never the case before It is impossible to ignore Him. It is quite possible to miss the full significance of His appeal. Every man has an interest in Him; but it is not every man whose interest issues in true knowledge. Says Dr Moffatt, in the Prologue to *Every man's Life of Jesus* · "Every man has an interest in Jesus. He may not know it. He may know it and yet he may not care enough about it. But for every man this is true, that life is not life, life cannot be all that God intended it to be, apart from Jesus." That is our contention. There is His attraction; in the fact that He brings to human life that which man can find no other way.

Here then is the claim we Christians dare to make; here is the challenge we throw out to the world. Our message is Jesus Christ and the claim is that this message is final and absolutely sufficient for man's utmost need. If we desire to bestow the greatest possible benefit on a fellow-man; if we wish to tell him the best news we possibly can tell, then, supposing that he has not heard before, we will tell him of Jesus Christ. For in the Gospel news, which is just the story of *Him* and all that He has done and is, man has "the answer to the world's greatest need."

Now what is there about Jesus Christ of Nazareth

that exercises such a complete fascination over the souls of men, captivates their hearts, wins their full allegiance, and holds them bound in willing bondage unto Him? It is probable that no two such willing slaves of Christ would give precisely similar answers to these queries. We might say at random—His teaching, His example, His life, His death, His victory—as Christians hold—over the grave's dread power. All these indeed are facets in the glowing gem of His attraction; yet we may hardly say that anyone of these comes first. At least it is necessary to give full emphasis to the one great fact which always hovers in the background and which illuminates the whole. We would lay utmost emphasis on our belief that it is *not* the case with Jesus that He came as Teacher, expounded His method of life, left a record of His system of conduct and departed as did Socrates or Buddha. It is much more than that. We point first of all to the Person of the Christ. We hold that He is the Incarnate Son of God; very God of very God. This it is which alters matters. Herein lies the very essence of the Christian message, and the only reason why we dare to make such sweeping claims for Him. It is the *Person* behind all the teaching and the acts that count. As a learned man has said, "As a historical fact, it is His Person, and not His method, that has overcome the world."[3] Thus it is that men become Christians because, as they obey His invitation "Come unto Me," and so learn of Him, they find themselves brought into touch with a living, all-powerful Personality. They have found Christ, or rather Christ has found them; and all life is changed.

Having emphasized that point, we may proceed to consider more in detail certain definite ways wherein the attraction of the Christ is felt. First let us put what we may call His unfailing capacity to deal with every case submitted to Him. In sober truth He has proved Himself "able to save to the uttermost." He can deal with any and every situation. His name "Jesus," being the shortened Greek form of "Joshua," means "the Lord saves." He is one who saves Thus when He lived in Palestine He went about saving people, saving them in body, soul and spirit. He healed the sick; He gave sight to the blind; He cheered the sad; He gave rest to the weary; He delivered the possessed; He proclaimed forgiveness to those burdened with their sins. The same holds good to-day, and will hold good for ever. He saves men now, saves their bodies, souls and spirits. He saves the *spirits* of us men. In Him we find forgiveness and so peace of mind. In Him we find too the spiritual strength needed to combat the powers of ill. He saves men's *bodies* too. Assuredly those who live in Him are in touch with an invigorating source of life and health. Still to-day in clear specific cases faith in Him has actually caused recovery of failing health. He saves men's *minds*. In truth *He* can "minister to a mind diseased." Particularly, various nervous ailments are often relieved, we might almost say are infallibly relieved, if only the sufferer will sufficiently trust Him and quietly "rest" in Him. Yes, because through prayer the patient finds himself in touch with Jesus Christ who still lives and who still says, "Come unto Me . . . and I will give you rest." Thus we would assert Christ Jesus is efficient and sufficient for every emergency. He satisfies the deepest needs of man Here is Someone who will never fail us men. However desperate may be our situation, He is sufficient for our needs. He is health and strength for body, mind and spirit.

How shall we attempt further to depict the perfection of our Christ and the utter satisfaction that we find in Him? Here is another theme for our consideration. We speak of *Prayer*. We know that the human soul is so composed that it requires to find an outlet for its heart's desires in prayer. Man, we are often reminded, is a religious animal; and he must find expression for the yearnings of his soul in prayer. We turn to Jesus Christ and ask "What has He to teach concerning prayer? How does He affect our prayers?" We answer that He has wrought a revolution in the art and rationale of true prayer. He has for one thing made it clear to us that we may expect with confidence answers to our prayers. He has in fact made prayer anew; He has transformed it; and He has done this by introducing into its method an element entirely new. For He has told mankind to pray to God the Father in His Name, the name of Jesus, Son of God. To prayer made in His Name men time and again have received clear answers such as strike the world as marvellous indeed. Here is an instance: "I travelled from Jerusalem, over 1,200 miles by motor to Persia, and saw there another angle in our prayer fellowship. I met the missionaries for whom you are praying, and learned there not only how much they depend upon our prayer help, but even more how much through prayer they are giving to us. Wherever I went there were prayer groups, and definite answers were the normal and expected result of a meeting. The day I arrived in Isfahan news had come of the illness of one of the missionaries. The Church met for prayer. The Persian pastor led intercessions by quietly reading over some of the promises of God. People prayed, mostly in Persian, men and women, and one saw this young Church growing in power through a daily experience of answered prayer. The next day came a telegram saying the missionary's temperature was normal. Some of us said, 'How wonderful.' The Persians quietly smiled and said, 'We expected it!'"[4] As we read, we too say, perhaps, "How wonderful"; or perhaps we smile at such simplicity of act and mind. Yet here is the plain fact that challenges our thought Those Christian men and women had offered prayer in Jesus' Name, and then received the answer, just as they expected. Prayer is a different thing since Jesus came and taught us how to pray. Effectual fervent prayer offered in His Name is the power men need for life.

Then His *Teaching* attracts. "Never man spake like this man," was the verdict of those sent in days of old to take Him into custody. This Man, who was so much more than man, spake and taught as none before or since has done. With *authority* He taught concerning many things; and it is just this element of authority and finality in His words which attracts and satisfies. His teaching is always up to date. All progress in moral knowledge and enlightenment is found to be simply a return to Him and what He said years and years ago. Here we touch upon a vitally important aspect of the Christian message. Herein the Gospel of Christ Jesus stands by itself in royal splendour midst all other systems of religion. This point was brought out very finely by the Archbishop of York, Archbishop Temple, speaking in York Minster in November, 1928. "Progress, if it is truly progressive, only illuminates the meaning of the Christian Gospel. In every generation there are two ways in which light comes. Sometimes it is found through the circumstances of life or the advance of secular knowledge. But when that happens it is always quickly found that the new light, far from being alien from the Gospel, was really shining in it all the while, and we were blind. Or else it is that from a fresh study of the Gospel men come to understand the teaching which hitherto had missed their attention, and then, acting upon that teaching, they see new light upon the problems of life. But always between the progress of man and the Gospel of Christ there is harmony and agreement. And most strikingly of all, so far as other religions in adaptation to the general movements of the world have themselves submitted to progress, it has been by moving away from the strict teaching of their founders. But for us, all progress is found in a return to Christ, and however far we move onwards we find that He is still our Leader, going on before us. And all this is true, because the directing principle of the Gospel is not a code but a spirit, and the focus of the Christian faith is not a formula, nor an experience, but is an actual Person who is Himself the living God."[5] Thus always our sufficiency is of Him. How attractive this is! How restful to know that here is One Whose teaching and guidance men of all ages and all nations may accept and ever find therein the satisfaction of their heart's desires, the guiding star to illuminate their highest hopes and dearest thoughts. However far we may advance in spiritual development and true progress, we never reach the point where we leave Him behind. Take as a specific instance His teaching about the nature and the heart of God. The God of Jesus is a God so full of love that no word save "Father" can express the truth. "Father,"—with this word Christ Jesus taught men to begin their prayers. This was *the* title by which the children of the human race were henceforth to speak to the Eternal Creator of the world. "True religion is falling in love with God," so we have been told. If this seems difficult at first to realize and follow out, let us see God as Christ Jesus has revealed Him to us. It is quite possible to fall in love with the God about whom Jesus spake. Love is seen to be an attribute of God to a degree not clearly realized before. This must be admitted; for before Christ Jesus, this Person "Who is Himself the living God," came and lived and died, there was no *Cross* for us to gaze upon. Now in the Cross of Calvary we see set forth the love of God, and upon the shadow of the Mount of Sinai there shines the light of Calvary's hill. The necessary truths of God's justice and demand of obedience from man are illumined by the revelation of His love. High up on the mount of fear, we see as taught by Christ the sign of love. Some years ago a party of travellers visited the district of Mount Sinai.

As the travellers approached their goal, the Convent of St. Catherine near Mount Horeb, the sun was setting and the glory of its dying rays lit up hill and valley. "Then, suddenly, as we passed on, we caught sight of a cross, set up on the height of Horeb; clear it stood against the sky, as if to show that love had conquered, and that none could ever come again in fear to 'the mount that burned with fire.'"[6] Yes, in the Cross of Jesus Christ love has conquered. Fear is cast out; love reigns.

To leave the subject of His teaching and consider the example of His Life; here too we find a beauty and unassailable uniqueness which surely must compel our admiration. Did ever man *act* like this? Did ever man come so humbly into the world, and say, "I am among you as He that serveth," and then *live* that saying out day after day? Consider further the sheer *kindness* of His acts, the sympathy, the insight He displayed. Call to mind those occasions when He went out of His way to do the kind thing, when, for instance, He healed the ear of Malchus in the garden, and when He prayed for His torturers whilst they bound Him to the Cross. "Father, forgive; Father, forgive them; they know not what they do." In that act and in those words millions have found an irresistibly attractive power. Here is a case in point: "When the notorious Japanese criminal, Tokichi Ishii, received the New Testament in his prison cell at Tokyo he placed it unopened upon a shelf, and at first gave no heed to the lady missionaries whom afterwards he learned to regard as 'the parents of my new life.' But one day, 'just for the sake of putting in the time,' he took the book down and read until some words of Christ smote him. 'I was stabbed to the heart as if by a five-inch nail,' he says. 'By the power of that one word of Christ's, *Father, forgive them; for they know not what they do*, my unspeakably hardened heart was changed and I repented of all my crimes '"[7] Yes, the manner in which He died, praying for those who slew Him, triumphing even in His agony, draws us unto Him. Consider the marvel of that death!

> "Was ever battle won like this—
> Where he that lost was gaining;
> And He that fell was triumphing,
> And He that died was reigning·
> And He that held the reed of scorn
> A sceptre was obtaining?"[8]

There is still one other aspect of His personality wherein we who follow Jesus find an infinite attraction. The *Claims* He makes upon His followers are in themselves a great attraction. He claims to be our Master; He claims our service and uttermost devotion. He asks that we give to Him ourselves, our bodies, souls and spirits. There is a magnetic spell in the royal splendour of our Master's call Those wise words of Dr. Hort deserve the thoughtful attention of us all, "It was not as an Example but as a Master that Christ spell-bound the Apostles."[9] Exactly. He bids us follow; and we follow gladly. He calls us to obey His orders; and we answer blithely to the call. He bids us go, and be, and do, and dare for Him; and freely, willingly, we show ourselves His servants day by day. And lo! in the very state of *service* there is *freedom* utter and complete. His service we find is perfect freedom. To serve Him is to reign. In submission unto Him men find themselves as happy and as free as kings!

Behold then the beauty of Messiah! See the attraction of His character and work, and claims! Yield to the spell of His magnetic personality, and so find in Him the satisfaction of your utmost needs.

"Our message is Jesus Christ." Without Him we cannot live, and we cannot bear to think of others living without Him—Jesus Christ the Saviour of the world, Jesus Christ the true Messiah, Jesus Christ the perfect Man, who is Himself the living God.

THIRD PART

DIFFICULTIES AND QUESTIONS.

Teach me Thy way, O LORD.
                    (Ps. lxxxvi. 11.)

Chapter X.

THE TRINITY IN UNITY.

ALTHOUGH I believe the cause of the rejection of Jesus to be primarily psychological and ethical—His demands being greater than most people of any race are prepared to accept—yet there are other considerations which have much weight with members of the Jewish nation.

These are, in particular, the difficulties they feel with regard to the Christian doctrine of God, and the attitude of Christians towards the Law of Moses. This and the next chapter will deal with the former, the two following chapters with the latter subject.

The Christian doctrine of God, *i.e.* the doctrine of the Trinity in Unity, is in Jewish eyes the most prominent feature of the Christian Faith.

Now we Christians believe that there is one God, and one God only, at least as strongly as do the Jews. Naturally I am not ignorant that in certain forms of Christianity worship is paid to the Blessed Virgin Mary (a merely human being) in such strong terms as almost to imply divinity. But the more thoughtful even among such worshippers do not in reality mean to attribute divinity to her, however strongly worded their prayers and praises may be. In any case a Jew must not suppose that worship of that kind forms any part of Christianity as such.

For us Christians the sentence *The LORD our God is one LORD* (Deut. vi. 4; Mark xii. 29) is the very foundation of our Faith, and any theological theory that contradicts it we detest and abhor. We affirm with every intellectual power we possess, and we believe with all our heart and soul, that there is one God and one God only. To think that there is more than one God is to stultify reason and revelation. Let that be quite clear

It is true that we speak of Three *Persons*, but in this connexion the word "Person" is not identical in meaning with "person" in our colloquial usage. When we say that we saw three persons in a certain place we mean three separate individuals, wholly distinct from each other, though all share a common humanity. That is not what is meant when we speak of the doctrine of the Trinity. Every educated man knows that the word "Person" is inadequate to express the thought intended, but that, unfortunately, no other and better word exists. "Person" usually suggests finality, with individuality closed to the outside, and that is not intended. "Personification" is clearly insufficient; "aspect" is too vague. Theologians are at a loss for a suitable definition. What it means in general terms is that God Himself is but one Person—as we should say—but that in that one Person (in the fullest sense of the word) there are three permanent sides, aspects—one is at a loss for terms—each of which has Its (or rather His) own function, supplementing, and being supplemented by, those of the other two.

But the Jews say that we Christians have made

THE TRINITY IN UNITY

"a compromise with heathenism."[1] They do not mean that Christians have consciously tried to run with the hare and hunt with the hounds, in other words, to combine monotheism with polytheism, for that would be simply an error. Nothing was further from the intention of the Church Fathers than an intentional compromise. They knew only too well by experience what polytheism was and did. They were monotheists heart and soul. If, on the other hand, it means that quite unintentionally the final Christian formula of faith is a mixture of Jewish and heathen ideas, this, though intelligible from the Jewish standpoint, is also mistaken. The Christian doctrine of the Trinity differs completely and fundamentally from any form of heathenism.

Let me first state what I believe to be the Jewish doctrine. If I am inaccurate my Jewish friends will correct me, bearing in mind that I am trying to represent the doctrine of Judaism as a whole, not that of any one party in it.[2]

What then is the Jewish doctrine of God? Many learned tomes have been written in definition and explanation. Here the statement must perforce be limited to a few lines.

There is one God, one God only, in need of nothing outside Himself. He is unique, incomparable, One. He is Father of the whole universe of sentient beings whom He created or is creating, but there is no being to whom the title Son can be given in any supreme and unique sense. His Spirit is little more than a synonym for His influence, or perhaps I should say, for His active work in the human heart (Psa. li. 11 [13]).

He is One and indivisible, not compound in any sense whatever.

His attributes are all that human reason and emotion can desire. He is perfect righteousness, perfect wisdom, perfect love. For Judaism does not conceive of God as does Mohammedanism, which (at least in its popular form, and, for all I know, in its scientific form also) regards God as Lord, almost identical with Fate, without love for His creatures, and without sympathy for them.

The God of Judaism is far different. No terms can be too strong to express His Fatherly love and providential care for every man. Members of the race of Abraham must be the last to doubt His providence, notwithstanding their sufferings.[3]

Jews, however, in their expositions and even in their prayers, go beyond this general conception of God, and frame their language in the hope of excluding anything approaching Christian phraseology. This they not unnaturally often misunderstand, and the result is that to us Gentiles the Jewish conception of God often seems to be made up more of negation than of affirmation. We Gentile Christians are therefore inclined to credit Judaism with something much more akin to sheer Mohammedanism than is really the case.

What then is the Christian doctrine of God? The fact that there is one God, one God only, is assumed throughout. But He is credited with being Life in its fullest sense, and containing *within Himself* all that makes up life, both cause and object. In Him are all the attributes that can possibly exist. Cause,

THE TRINITY IN UNITY

Object, and That which unites are all in Him. Thus He does not need any one, much less any thing, te satisfy Himself, for He combines all in Himself. Ho is the Cause, He is the Result, He is that which brings the Result about. He is thus (shall we say?) Threefold—not that each "fold" is distinct or separate— yet He is One God and one God only.

You say, I do not understand this.

Of course you do not. Is it likely that we should understand God? We do not understand ourselves. In each of us are (as we say) body, soul and spirit. Do we, can we, understand our relation to each "part"? A man dare not say I have a body, I have a soul; I have a spirit. For he is—not has—body, soul and spirit. We do not understand this, and never shall in this life. But we affirm it, and, in a sense, know it. So with our faith in the Trinity, which primarily is Unity. We affirm our belief in the Trinity in Unity.

A reader, however, will say: "But I cannot get over the difficulty of there being a Son. How can God have a Son?"

I answer: You will observe that it is not the term "Son" to which you object. For you quite accept the term "son of God." *Israel is My son*, says the LORD in Exod. iv. 22. And in Hosea He says: *When Israel was a child, then I loved him, and called My son out of Egypt* (xi. 1). So Israelites are His *sons* (Deut. xiv. 1). And He addresses David (according to most Jewish expositors, and perhaps rightly), as, *Thou art My Son* (Ps. ii. 7). Further, as it seems, angels are called *sons of God* (Job i. 6; ii. 1; xxxviii. 7). So it is not the phrase *son of God* in itself to which my

Jewish readers object. Their objection lies in our using the term Son in the special sense of what we call Second "Person" in the Trinity, and they laugh and say: "How can God have a Son?" For they seem to think that we attribute to God an action in time that corresponds in some measure with the sexual relation of man and woman. If we did mean anything of the kind the Jewish objection would be well-founded indeed.

But of course we mean nothing of the sort. Did the prophets attribute any such act to the LORD when they said Israel was His Son? Did the psalmist, who even adds, *This day have I begotten thee* (Ps. ii. 7)? Whatever the primitive ideas may have been, by the days of the prophets in Israel all carnal lineage had long since been put aside, and relationship of soul and spirit was alone in mind. And such "sonship" could, after all, at best (even though only of soul and spirit, and not of body) be but partial and imperfect. The "Sonship" of the Second Person in the Trinity is also wholly spiritual, yet is also perfect and complete. He is more truly "Son" than any other "son," of man, or of God.

It may, however, be asked: Why have Christians given so ambiguous a name as Son to the Second Person in the Trinity?

One reason is that we can think of no better term. An ideal "Son" surely is he who ideally represents his "Father," and as we understand the Second Person in the Trinity to be the perfect representative of the First—alas, that we must use human terms to express Divine things, but we have none but human language—

so "Son" expresses what we mean, as exactly as our human language permits.

Another reason is that Jesus spoke of Himself as the Son of God in an unique sense, and we follow His nomenclature, not slavishly indeed, but, as we have seen, because we cannot improve upon it.

The objection may be raised—Where do you find all this in the Old Testament? What evidence do you discover there for belief in the Second Person of the Trinity? We cannot see any text even in the Holy Writings, or in the Prophets, and much less in the Law, which certainly speaks of Him.

To speak quite frankly—and in this book I desire to be absolutely honest and straightforward—it seems to me to be of very little importance whether there is even one such text in the Hebrew Bible or not. For, as the whole tenor of this book has shown, we Christians do not believe, and ought not to believe, in the Lord Jesus because of the Old Testament, but we believe, and ought to believe, in the Old Testament because we believe in Him.

We are drawn to Jesus for what He was and is, and then we gratefully and gladly turn to the Hebrew Bible and find that it only confirms our Faith.

But this confirmation, as I have tried to say again and again, does not depend on predictions, but on the one great moral purpose running all through the Hebrew Bible. Its hope and aim are carried out to the full in Jesus—so far as they can be fulfilled in any one individual. If indeed the Hebrew Bible anywhere contradicted our Christian Faith it would be another and a very serious matter. But no Jew, however ingenious, can find a single text in the Old Testament that contradicts the Christian Faith intelligently understood. We Christians therefore glory in the Hebrew Bible, and make it our own, and indeed claim that by its purpose and hope it belongs to us even more than to the Jews. They, we believe, have failed to obey it, being satisfied with its more apparent and superficial teaching. Its kernel is ours, and we *magnify the Law and make it honourable.*

Someone, again, will ask: What about the Third Person, Him whom you call in archaic English the Holy Ghost, *i.e.* the Holy Spirit. There are, no doubt, many references to the Spirit of God in the Hebrew Bible, but why say that this is a "Person"? We Jews believe that the term means a mere influence, or, perhaps rather, a synonym for the One God in the exercise of His grace and love?

Although it is not very probable that he who accepts the doctrine of the Second Person in the Godhead will boggle at that of the Third, yet a few words must be said. Why do we believe the Holy Ghost to be a Person and not a mere influence? One reason is that (if we consider the question) He rounds off, so to say, the doctrine of the Trinity. There is the Father and there is the Son, and, as it were, joining them together, is the Holy Spirit, who thus becomes distinguished from all merely spiritual influences, and from all creatures however spiritual they may be.

It is not probable, however, that the early believers argued in this way. We can hardly doubt that they were guided by the language of the writers of the New Testament, and the words of the Lord Jesus Himself.

THE TRINITY IN UNITY

In the first place we find phrases used of the Holy Ghost which imply personality rather than influence, e.g. *Jesus was led . . . by the Spirit* (Matt. iv. 1); *The Spirit of your Father which speaks in you* (Matt. x. 20); *The Holy Spirit shall teach you in that day* (Luke xii. 12). Similarly St. Paul says that when we pray the Spirit intercedes, and has a mind of His own (Rom. viii. 26 *seq.*). Above all, instead of a neuter pronoun being used—as we should expect for the grammatical agreement—a masculine pronoun is sometimes expressly used of Him (John xiv. 26; xv. 26; xvi. 7, 13 *seq.*).

Partly then by logic, and partly by deference to the terms used in the New Testament, the early Church perceived that the Holy Spirit was a Person and not an influence. So at the end of the Gospel according to St. Matthew we find Him placed on an equality with the Father and the Son (of course in the Unity of the One God), for the Lord Jesus Christ bids His followers *make disciples of all the nations, baptizing them into the name of the Father and of the Son and of the Holy Spirit* (Matt. xxviii. 19).

A Jewish reader may ask—perhaps with just a touch of impatience in his voice—Yes, yes, but what of the Old Testament? We should like you to prove the personality of the Holy Ghost from the Hebrew Bible. No doubt. But if the argument of this book is sound we have no right to expect to find in the Old Testament any such proof. And indeed, though many texts in the Old Testament have been adduced by Christian controversialists as proofs (in the strictest sense of the term) of the personality of the Holy Ghost, there is not one of such proof-texts that is (without legitimate doubt) sufficient for this purpose. Personally I am sure we are not justified in expecting to find one. The time for the revelation of this truth had not then come.

But I ask you to observe this. The phrase *the Spirit of God*, or *the Spirit of the LORD*, or perhaps its equivalent, occurs hundreds of times in the Hebrew Bible, and in no case does it exclude the thought of personality. In other words, although the Hebrew Bible nowhere directly and certainly teaches the personality, its language is invariably consistent with our Christian doctrine.

The treatment of the Hebrew Bible by us Christians with reference to the Holy Spirit is, in fact, much the same as the treatment of it by Jews with reference to the Oral Law. As point after point in the Oral Law is not due to the Hebrew words, but when it has been seen has then found support (more or less close) in the Hebrew, so Christians, having learned a truth about the Holy Spirit, find, to their heart's content, support (again more or less close) in the language of the Old Testament. Nor can we wonder at this. For Holy Scripture, Old as well as New, is given by inspiration of God, God overruling what has been written.

Chapter XI.

THE INCARNATION.

Jews say that they cannot believe in the Incarnation; that the supposition that Jesus was God is repulsive to them. So at the risk of repetition something must be said with immediate reference to this difficulty.

It is hardly necessary to say that many of the objections found in medieval Jewish writers are due to a misunderstanding of the Christian doctrine, a misunderstanding which is in great part a reaction from popular ignorance on the side of the Christians

For in those days Christians laid so much stress on the Divinity of the Lord Jesus as almost to efface the truth of His Humanity.

Hence Jews could ask, as we may see in their writings again and again, How can God pray to God? How can God be weary? How can God be crucified? And there are many other questions of the same kind, all alike due to failure to understand what the doctrine of the Incarnation means. For it does not mean that God became Man only in appearance. It is something very much more than that. If Jesus was God, and only added to Himself manhood with the weakness of a human body and a certain amount of human intelligence—if that is all the Incarnation means, the objection is valid. It would be impossible for "God" to pray to God.

But the Incarnation means much more than this. It means the submerging (if I may say so) of the Divine in the Human. It means that God really did become man, and that as incarnate He ceased to function as God. Never mind the difficulties of such a belief for the moment. Let us get hold of, and understand, what the Christian doctrine is. It is that God took human nature in its fulness. This does not mean that a Divine Person dwelt in a man, and that sometimes the God acted and sometimes the Man. Perish the thought! That would indeed be a monstrosity, neither God nor Man but a queer mixture of both, of no possible value to us as an Example, and of no possible value in the eyes of the universe as a real Mediator. No, the Incarnation is far wider and deeper. It means that until Jesus was born there was no one in the world who entirely answered to God's purpose in Creation, and also that in Jesus God took and glorified humanity in perfection.

The fact is that there is a tendency in human nature to draw a sharper distinction between God and Man than is warranted by Scripture. True, that God said to Moses: *Thou canst not see My face: for man shall not see Me and live* (Exod. xxxiii. 20). For evidently human eyes are fitted for the things of this material universe only. And human intelligence is limited by the convolutions of the physical brain. So there can be no question of the inability of a man to see the blaze of the Divine Glory either physical or intellectual or (as one need hardly say) spiritual. We therefore cannot see God and live. And yet the prophet Ezekiel might have reminded us that we must not make a final distinction between the two terms.[1] Manhood and Deity are not real, but only verbal and partial, antitheses.

While, however, Jews quite naturally shrink from the doctrine of the Incarnation, even in the true meaning and implications of the term, they even more naturally find a difficulty in its mode, as it has been accepted by the Church. For the very early Apostles' Creed, which is recited by the great majority of believers, contains the clause, "Born of the Virgin Mary."

Now we dare not say that belief in the Virgin Birth of the Lord Jesus is a *sine quâ non* of the Christian Faith. For there is no evidence that it formed part of the earliest proclamation of the Gospel. Probably most of the converts, Jewish and Gentile, in the first forty years after the Crucifixion knew nothing of it

Yet in itself it is antecedently more probable than the supposition that the Lord Jesus had a human father. For then the Logos can only have been joined to a specific human person, and each person—the Divine and the human—would have been independent, forming the monstrosity to which reference has already been made. On *a priori* grounds the Virgin Birth is the more probable.

As to physical difficulties we know too little to make confident assertions. It is a mistake, no doubt, to lay much stress on the apparent fact that there are rare cases of parthenogenesis in Nature. The present writer, at least, has not sufficient knowledge of biology to be able to estimate the accuracy, or the value, of the statement. Yet for the supreme revelation of God through matter, God might be expected to choose the finest and holiest medium at His disposal. And though the doctrine of the Immaculate Conception of the Blessed Virgin was not a part of the official creed of Roman Catholics till 1851 (and the New Testament suggests, on the other hand, that she was not faultless), yet it is a reasonable belief that she was the most perfect, and the least sinful, of any descendant of Adam until the Blessed Son was born.

Personally I am convinced that the feeling of Christians has been right in holding the doctrine of the Virgin Birth of the Lord Jesus.

Some one, however, may ask: Why this hesitation? How can there be any doubt at all, when St. Matthew, after relating the words of the angel to Joseph about the promised Birth, adds: *Now all this is come to pass, that it might be fulfilled which was spoken by the Lord through the prophet, saying, Behold, the virgin shall be with child, and shall bring forth a son, and they shall call his name Immanuel* (Matt. i. 22 *seq.*; Isa. vii. 14)? Does not that make it clear, he asks, that the author of the First Gospel understood the words in Isaiah to be a direct and infallible statement that the Messiah was to be born of a virgin? No, it does not. For, as every learned Jew (be he Christian or not) is well aware, St. Matthew may be only quoting the Old Testament passage by way of illustration, without committing himself, or indeed paying much attention, to the question what the original and proper meaning of the passage might be. To this method of quotation we have already referred in an earlier chapter.[2] The author of the First Gospel may or may not have had the

Hebrew text in mind. He certainly knew the oldest
Jewish translation of it that we possess. For the old
Greek version which we call the Septuagint translates
the Hebrew word in question by *parthenos*, "virgin."
And this translation is almost certainly right in this
passage. For translation is not a matter of expressing
the meaning of a bare word in itself, taken out of its
context. If that is all that is required, then Aquila's
translation *neanis*, "a young woman," is doubtless
correct. But a good translator does much more than
that. He considers a whole passage, and "virgin"
does give the meaning intended by Isaiah. For when
Isaiah is wishing to encourage Ahaz he tells him that
before a certain young unmarried woman bears the
child, the land shall be set free from its foes. And the
Septuagint translator saw the point, and by using
"virgin" made it clear that she was still unmarried.
For thus it was plainer than ever that the Deliverance
was to be brought about by God, and the Child could
rightly be called Immanuel, *i.e.* God with us.

But you say: This is no proof of the Virgin Birth of
Jesus! I never said it was. But I do say that
St. Matthew found in the phrase a fitting illustration
of the fact he already knew and desired to emphasize.
For he held strongly that God overruled all that was
written, and he rejoiced to see in Holy Scripture a
verbal confirmation of the truth that he himself held
dear, the Birth of the Lord Jesus from the Blessed
Virgin.[3]

Chapter XII.

THE NON-OBSERVANCE OF THE LAW—IN GENERAL.

How can Christians be right in saying that the Law is abolished, and therefore is not to be observed?

What is meant to be understood by the term the Law, *i.e.* the Torah? For writers often forget that the term on the lips of a Jew has two meanings, one of which is of much broader content than the other. In its broader sense Torah is to all intents and purposes identical with "religion," *viz.* the religion of Judaism, with all that this includes, both the written Law and the Oral Law, as developed down to our own day, with all the ceremonies and observances required of the conscientious and instructed Jew How far indeed Torah includes doctrinal religion, *i.e.* doctrine as contrasted with practice, may be questioned, and, in any case is not of great importance. For to a Jew, practice is of greater value than theory, and he may believe what he likes if he only conforms to Jewish practice.

In the narrower sense of the word, Torah (the Law) refers only to the Pentateuch, which, as every one knows, stands on a pedestal far higher than the rest of the Hebrew Bible. For to Jews the three volumes of the Bible are (*a*) the Law, *i.e.* the Pentateuch; (*b*) the Prophets, whether Former (Joshua, Judges,

Samuel and Kings), or Latter (Isaiah, Jeremiah, Ezekiel, with the Book of the Twelve, our "minor prophets"); (c) the Writings, i e. all the remaining books, ending with Chronicles. These volumes have three grades of "inspiration." The first, the Law proper, is inspired through and through, every word and indeed every letter being the direct result of the speech of God. The second (the Prophets) is also highly inspired, but not so highly as the Law. The third (the Writings) are indeed also somewhat inspired, in very varying degree. Hence "proof" for any observance or belief found in the Writings is of comparatively little weight; in the Prophets is to be considered with respect; but only in the Law does it form strong and convincing evidence. The Pentateuch, and the Pentateuch alone, is the final court of appeal. If a doctrine is not to be found there Jews need not accept it. That was what the Sadducees felt about the Resurrection, and therefore it was that our Lord brought forward His proof from Exod. iii. 6 (Mark xii. 26), even as in the third century of the Christian era Pharisees, arguing on the same lines in favour of the doctrine, adduced as proof, Deut. xi. 9: *the land which the LORD sware unto your fathers to give unto them.* "It is not said to *you*, but to *them*. Hence the doctrine of the resurrection of the dead is found in the Law."[1]

But this Law, the Pentateuch, what is it? It contains orders to do so-and-so, and not to do so-and-so, and such orders amount to no less than six hundred and thirteen.[2] In itself the word *Torah* means "direction." See Hag. ii. 11, where, in answer to requests for such direction, the priests point out that *holy flesh* does not spread holiness to other objects, but *one that is unclean by a dead body* does spread uncleanness. Hence it is of extreme importance to every Jew to learn exactly what each ordinance of the Torah, each positive and each negative commandment, means, and precisely to what objects it refers. Here the Oral Law steps in, and the Talmud gives an account of many of the discussions held by the Rabbis as they fixed and developed the Oral Law up to their time. For the process still continues. For example, it is hardly determined even to-day whether Jews are allowed to eat caviare or not. For caviare is the roe of the sturgeon, and it is questionable whether the sturgeon has the necessary scales and fins to make it clean (Lev. xi. 9–12). For scientists point out that its scales and fins are not like those of most fishes, but are in reality merely bones. If so, it has not scales and fins in the strictest sense, and the sturgeon and all its products are an abomination. If this be so, then, of course, caviare is forbidden to a Jew.

This then is the Law; a collection of statutes given by God, and therefore, in Jewish eyes, to be reverently received and obeyed. Whether the reasons for enactment are perceived in every case makes no difference. Some Jewish writers have even insisted that the less intelligible God's commands are, the greater reason there is for following them. He is absolute Monarch, and can order what He chooses; man must only obey.

Now, apart from Christian arguments as such, and, particularly without taking the teaching of the New Testament into consideration, we twentieth-century folk feel difficulties about this minute obedience to Pentateuchal legislation, and its corollaries in the Oral Law. For parts of it, to say the very least, seem to us (pardon the term) barbaric. Is not circumcision a barbarous rite? Is it not ghastly to sacrifice goats, sheep and bulls, so ghastly indeed that it is doubtful if, when the new Temple is built at Jerusalem, the majority of Jews then living will be in favour of renewing the sacrificial system. Even the dietary laws too, in so far as they do not depend on hygiene (as some of them ultimately do), represent to modern minds very primitive and uncivilized notions, especially when they are due (as it seems) to anxiety lest the Jews should fall into heathen forms of worship.[3]

But for a strict Jew all such regulations are alike binding; and though some Jews are not strict, and take it upon themselves (either individually or in communities of smaller or greater size) to determine what portions of the Law they shall and shall not observe, yet no coherent principle seems to underlie their choice. Categorically, then, the Law, the whole Law, claims obedience to every one of its precepts. This is, of course, not to say that in some sense one precept may not be of greater moral importance than another, but Jews feel that we frail and ignorant men have no meteyard by which to determine importance, and that all God's precepts therefore must be obeyed equally.

It may, or rather must, be asked: How is it then—if the Jews claim that implicit obedience be given to the Law—that Christians disregard it? For this attitude of Christians, we must remember, is no new thing. The situation is not like that of certain Christian doctrines which did not take form until three or four centuries had passed. This negation of the Law as not binding upon Gentile believers, nor even in strictest theory upon believers from among the Jews, belongs to the earliest Christian times It is plain enough in Christian documents of the sixth and seventh decades of the first century. It appears also in other documents which took their present form in the eighth and ninth decades, but are compiled from much earlier materials. Those primitive Christians believed that the observance of the Law was not binding upon them. How was this?

We have seen that to people who enjoy the civilization of the twentieth century some of the enactments of the Law seem barbaric. But there is no trace of this feeling among the early Christians. Why then did they repudiate the Law? They were not told to do so by the Master. No doubt, He said that certain specified commands might be, and ought to be, neglected in the sense in which they were commonly understood. But He did not expressly say that the Law as such was not to be observed. Why then, I ask again, was it repudiated?

One answer, as I believe, lies in the Old Testament itself.[4] The Hebrew Bible points to the supersession of the Law in the meaning that was usually given to it. Far be it from me to adduce any of those crass and medieval conceptions of Old Testament prophecies to which reference has been already made. God forbid that I should so profane that holy scholarship we now enjoy.

Yet the Holy Writings plainly indicate a higher form of devotion to the LORD than sacrifices as such suggest. The psalmist, for example, says: *Sacrifice and offering thou hast no delight in, ears hast Thou hollowed out for me. Burnt offering and sin offering hast Thou not required. Then said I, Lo, I am come . . . I delight to do Thy will, O my God, yea, Thy law is within my inmost parts* (Psa. xl 6–8). Not mere sacrifices, he says, but bodily ears wherewith to hear Thy commands, and then to perform them from the innermost soul—these indeed form Thy true service.

The date when this psalm was written is of no matter for our immediate purpose. Indeed, no one can be sure of the precise age either of our psalter as a whole, or of any of its five books, or indeed of a single one of its poems. It is no more possible to determine when a particular psalm was written than to discover from a modern hymn book alone the date of the composition of any given hymn. We may find this out from external evidence, but in the case of the psalter no certain evidence exists. Fortunately, for our general purpose, the date of this or that psalm is of no importance. We may have our private opinions, and indeed every conscientious student must have his own, but we cannot say more.

Yet what does the psalter say about true religion? Is not the LORD to the psalmists no mere Giver of external laws and precepts, but the Giver of laws and precepts devised to further the highest spiritual instincts of His own people, and indeed of all nations outside the revelation so far made to Israel (see, for example, Psa. xxii. 27)? The intense spiritual life revealed in the Psalms suggests that the literal obedience to orders ostensibly referring to material and external things is already losing its value, as not possessing permanent worth.

What then of the Prophets? When Jeremiah wrote: *Behold the days come, saith the LORD, that I will make a new covenant with the house of Israel, and with the house of Judah, etc.* (Jer. xxxi. 31–34), he did not intend to refer to the volume of the New Testament in contrast with that of the Old. Nor did he speak of the Gospel as though it were a new "Law." In fact no merely verbal prediction lies in his utterance. What he probably meant was that the Law which had been given by God to Israel was to be new in this sense, that in the future it was to be understood aright, and be received into the heart, and lived out. For that, it seems, is how the Law had always been intended to be treated.[5]

Now this is important, for more reasons than one.

It is the very antithesis to the belief of many scholars that the prophets repudiated the sacrificial system. The words of Amos: *Did ye bring unto Me sacrifices and offerings in the wilderness forty years, O house of Israel* (v. 25), have been misunderstood, as though the prophet meant to say that God had not ordered sacrifices at all; that they were in fact contrary to His express desire. This opinion is closely connected with the suppositions that the really great teachers of Israel were the prophets alone, and that the cult with its many sacrifices, bloody and unbloody, and its consequent insistence on the meritorious value of their due performance, was only the result of a form of

Judaism posterior to, and decadent from, the purer teaching of the prophetic order. Nothing can be more false than this under-estimation of the age of the sacrificial system in general. This is not, it will be noticed, a literary question. Wellhausen may be right in dating the Pentateuch, in the form that we know it, as late as the fifth century before the common era. That may, or may not, be true, and, in any case, throws no light at all upon the date of the sacrificial cult in general. The theory that when the prophets wrote they were attacking a recent outbreak of external religion, and believed that in Israel of old there were virtually no such things as sacrifices, is to run counter to all the probabilities of history, and to the evidence of the Old Testament itself. For primitive religion (so far as we yet know it) always had sacrifices, and held that their performance in due ritual was a matter of primary importance. If so, to place high and spiritual teaching first, and crass externalism afterwards, is contrary to the analogy of early religions.

And the Old Testament bears this out. The Pentateuch as we have it may be late. But no scholar doubts that many of its contents are early. And, according to it, sacrifices existed from the very first. Cain's and Abel's sacrifices represent facts in that primitive religion with which the religion of Israel was closely connected. And so with all the sacrifices mentioned in the book of Genesis. Similarly, there is no doubt that there were sacrifices in the times of the Judges and of the Kings. Such sacrifices formed part of Israel's religion from its earliest history.

The fact is that the prophets found a system of

sacrifices already in existence, and tending to become more elaborate with each generation, and they further found that the greater part of the people were inclined to lay so much stress on the due performance of these sacrifices that this was regarded as making up for the lack of true spiritual life, and even for vile sins. Let there be no more sacrifices of this kind, cry the prophets. Of what value is the mere trampling in the courts of the LORD? Attend to moral duties (Isa. 1. 11–17, cf. Hagg. ii. 14). In other words, the prophets call for observance of the real character of the religion given to Israel by God. The whole Law, they seem to say, is penetrated by the highest possible ethical thought, and to be satisfied with less is to fail to grasp its purpose and intention.

What then of the Law itself, the Law in its narrower meaning of the Pentateuch? Is there no evidence that it was intended to impress spiritual truths upon the nation in the degree that people were able to bear them? Can any one suppose that the elaborate description of the tabernacle and its furniture—to say nothing of the detailed regulations about the sacrifices themselves—had no ulterior object than that of merely chronicling the LORD's orders? *See that thou make them after their pattern, which hath been shewed thee in the mount* (Exod. xxv. 40).

This is usually, and rightly, understood to mean that the LORD did not show Moses a mere sketch or plan of what he was to make, but a vision of a tabernacle *in the Mount*. Was that material? Or, if it was material in some sense, for we can well suppose that in "heaven" there is matter of a kind, yet its spiritual character and being must have been all-important. So with the building that, as we are told, Moses erected. Its spiritual meaning must have been in sight from the very first. Nor indeed should we expect otherwise from an Oriental people, inclined to parable and imagery. Why say that certain hangings should be blue, and others scarlet, and so on, if the variety of colour did not represent moral and spiritual truths? Why insist on the sacred numbers three and seven, and combinations of three and four, etc., etc., if to do so were only to indicate to the thoughtful student of Oriental mathematical lore the importance of system and order in things appertaining to God or man? No doubt, absurd interpretations of details in Exodus, Numbers and Leviticus, have often been given by careless and unscholarly, even though devout, persons But mistakes do not destroy truth. They do but make us more painstaking students of the Divine narrative. The various enactments, even to details, do possess a spiritual signification for those whose eyes have been enlightened, and understand something of the Oriental mind.

How does this affect the question before us, *viz.* by what right do believers in the Lord Jesus repudiate the observance of the Law? Plainly enough. For their desire is to observe the Law in its primary intention. If the spiritual, and not the material, is the real aim and purpose of the Law, then they best keep the Law and magnify it, *and make it honourable* (Isa. xlii. 21) who do everything possible to carry out its purpose

Observe that there is no desire in these pages to suggest for one moment that Jews who protest their devotion to the Law think that external observance of the enactments is sufficient. To assert that is but to exhibit one's ignorance of Jewish lives. These do, in fact, put the lives of many Christians to shame. That is not the question. The question is: How is it that Christians repudiate the observance of the Law in its externals, and aim only at observing it in its spiritual, and therefore more important, aims and intentions?

Yet how do we know that this was its purpose? Partly, as has already been said, by the hints contained in the Writings, and the Prophets, and even the Pentateuch itself; and partly by the lessons of the life of the Lord Jesus. No one, as we have seen, in all history has been so perfect as He. Yet, though a Jew, and though He never formally repudiated the observance of the Law as a whole, He did by His teaching indirectly show that its enactments were not necessarily to be observed in the letter, if this militated against the observance of the spirit.

I have already quoted Jer. xxxi. 31-34. But notice what the last words in that quotation imply; nothing less than a complete change of motive in observing the Law. The time will come, says the prophet, when the forgiveness of sins will be the basis of keeping the Law, the foundation of a holy life, and not its summit and crown.

But this is the very opposite to the central teaching of Judaism as we know it to-day, and as it has been since the first century of our era, and in all probability since the earliest days of Judaism. For the idea of "merit" in obtaining life hereafter—merit in its lowest meaning of desert, in such a way that a good deed outweighs a bad one—plays so large a part in the natural feelings of men about religion, that it is always hard to be eradicated. But it is clear that if, as it seems, Jeremiah really meant that the knowledge of forgiveness by God is the true starting-point in running the race of carrying out His will, then the Law, as such, even without its hard and fast rules worked out to minutiæ by the conscientious efforts of generations of Jewish thinkers, has to come to an end, being superseded by the motive of doing what God has said, in its highest possible meaning and extent, in order to glorify Him. It will no longer be: Do this, do that, in order that you may obtain pardon and eternal life, but, Let me carry out Thy will, O Lord, for Thou hast already forgiven all my sins, and I am on a footing of intimate relationship with Thee.

So we are brought to the last and greatest reason why the Law as such is superseded, a reason which, alas, will not appeal to any Jew at all. It appeals to Christians, and indeed is to them the great reason of all. But if a Jew grants it he ceases to be a Jew at heart, and becomes a Christian. Yet I must state it here, in order that every Jewish reader may at least understand the argument, even though for many reasons he does not accept its validity.

The argument is as follows. The Law, meaning by this term now all the revelation which God has given of His will in the Writings, the Prophets and the Law proper, claims to be obeyed fully and perfectly. I am indeed well aware that Jewish writers are apt to say that God does not require so much as that, but is quite satisfied with only the average performance of His will by the average man. But that assertion can hardly be taken seriously. It is a light and frivolous phrase, which has, so far as I am aware, no support in Scripture, and rests only on a dim feeling that God cannot be too exacting. He will then be a mild-mannered personage, whose threats are not to be taken very seriously after all, but are not unlike the bug-a-boos of a fond mother, doing her best to save her children from doing themselves harm, and have not any substantial reality behind them.

But we cannot play with God like this. He says: *My judgments shall ye do, and My statutes shall ye keep, to walk therein: I am the LORD your God. Ye shall therefore keep My statutes and My judgments: which if a man do, he shall live in them. I am the LORD* (Lev. xviii. 4 *seq*). The promise may include, and probably does include, ordinary life on earth, but it refers chiefly to that which is really life, life connected with communion with Him whose name is repeated, *the LORD your God.*

Now observe what this implies: that unless a man does keep the revelation of God in its fulness, and as far as he understands it, he falls short of what God requires of him, either by omission or by commission, and must in the nature of things receive corresponding spiritual loss, such as, from another point of view, may be called punishment. I say "in the nature of things," because there is no arbitrariness in Nature or in God. "The mills of God" are also the mills of Nature, and may "grind slowly," but "they grind exceeding small." And there is no escape For God's honour, with which is bound up the honour of all Nature (the whole

Universe of existence) is one, and to stain it is to cry out for judgment. If so, how is escape possible? For *there is no man who sinneth not* (1 Kings viii. 46; *cf.* Prov. xx. 9; Eccles. vii. 20), and no amount of performance of good can make up for one act of evil, however insignificant it may seem.

The answer is that no escape is possible. The whole world lieth in sin, and each person in it is condemned. The impasse is hopeless. This much the Old Testament thunders forth to us, holding us down in the ring, however nimbly controversialists may try to jump over the ropes. Now comes the New Testament.

For, as we have already seen, this tells us of Jesus of Nazareth, in whose life no one has successfully found any sin at all, and whose death was a magnificent gesture of self-sacrifice. But, you say, can God and Nature and the whole Universe accept the sacrifice of any one man, even of a man completely perfect, in the stead of other men who are imperfect? Who has ever said that He can? Certainly no Christian. For the Christian, as we have seen, has found himself forced by logical thought to believe that Jesus of Nazareth is far more than man, even the One Very and Eternal God—no less. Not any man, however good, but God Himself, has broken through the impasse. That, and nothing less, is the Good News, the Gospel.

It must be freely confessed that the method by which God has accomplished this is still under discussion by Christian people, and almost certainly will be so discussed for all time No astonishment need be expressed, for precise knowledge of the interrelation of God and man must always be beyond us. The same kind of difficulty arises even about Old Testament statements. God created the world, we are told, and we do not doubt the fact. But can any Jew or Christian explain the method by which God did so? God spoke to Moses face to face (Exod. xxxiii. 11), and again we do not doubt it. Yet can any one say how it took place, what was the method of that revelation? No, we must be content to know as yet but little of God's methods, of the exact formulæ, so to speak, of the reagents combined in the alembic of His will.

It is, therefore, not in the least necessary to enquire into, or even to state, the various theories of the method of the Atonement. The essential and irreducible part of the doctrine is that God Himself brought about the Reconciliation at His own cost. In other words, that, in accordance with the fundamental teaching of even the Old Testament, self-sacrifice is the root and source of all deliverance of others. God's honour, which includes the honour of all Nature and the Universe, had been smirched, and God alone could wipe away the stain Himself, and at His own expense. There is no moral blame in self-sacrifice. God so loved the world that He gave Himself for it. This is the Christian doctrine, nothing less.

It may, however, be argued that the phrase "God so loved the world that He gave Himself for it" is not quite accurate. For in the Gospel according to St. John we read: *God so loved the world that He gave—not Himself—but—His only begotten Son* (John iii. 16). So He did not give Himself, but someone else! But we have already seen[6] that the Son is not a different individual from God. We must use human terms, but the Christian Faith—and at the moment we are describing what this is, and not what others may suppose it to be—holds tenaciously that the only-begotten Son is as much God as the "Father," and is not to be understood as a separate Being from Him. *Hear, O Israel, the LORD our God is one LORD* is as strong a Christian slogan as a Jewish. The words of John (iii. 16) tell us that God gave Himself in that permanent "aspect" (no word in human language can be accurate) in which He has always held communication with matter, and therefore with man, and enters thus into fellowship with human life, and thus becomes a spectacle to the whole universe, in His utter self-abandonment, self-abasement and humiliation. Love for man and creation even to the uttermost could alone wipe away the sin of man, and this God Himself accomplished once for all.[7]

After what may have seemed to be a long digression (but is no digression) we come back to the Law. Why then do Christians consider it superseded? Because it failed. It had no power to satisfy the final demands of holiness and righteousness. It could not cleanse from sin. Why then should we be bound by the Law? It was helpful, indeed necessary, in its time. But, as we have seen, it pointed forward to a better state of things, which has already come. It is therefore, for the Christian, only a retrogression to take it any longer as the final standard of holiness.

In fact we have a better standard. Jesus of Nazareth is, in life and word, a more perfect exponent, a far higher revelation, of the will and purpose of God than any number of written rules and regulations.

We Christians get glimpses, and far more than glimpses—splendid and gorgeous sun-rise glories—of God's will and character and purpose in the books of the Hebrew Bible, and he who rejects that source of spiritual knowledge is strangely foolish, not to say spiritually conceited. But that is all. The Old Testament can never be to a Christian more than a collection of broken glass, which, even if it were pieced together, would never make the lovely picture of God displayed in the Life and Death and Resurrection and Ascension of His only begotten Son, Jesus Christ our Lord.

CHAPTER XIII.

THE NON-OBSERVANCE OF THE LAW IN DETAIL: CIRCUMCISION, SABBATH, THE DIETARY LAWS.

So far we have considered the attitude of Christians to the Law in general. It remains to ask why particular parts of it are not observed? For though the answer to the general question in reality governs procedure in details, yet a specific reply may be helpful.

(1) *Circumcision.*

This naturally comes first among those specific parts of the Law which have been discarded by Christians. For it has always been considered to be of more importance than any other enactment. If, for example, it clashes with the Sabbath rest—for a child must be circumcised on the eighth day from its birth (Gen. xvii. 12)—it is the Sabbath that is "pressed down" by circumcision, and not vice versâ. This regulation is at least as early as the first century of our era (John vii. 23). The cause of this importance is, no doubt, that God gave the order to Abraham himself, the ancestor of the whole nation. To be sure, the Sabbath is mentioned in the second chapter of Genesis as having been made holy at the Creation. But, even so, the direct ordinance to observe it was not given before the time of Moses. Circumcision is therefore of greater importance both religiously and nationally than any other specific duty. Why then do Christians, even Christians belonging to the Jewish race, not observe it?

It has indeed been suggested that as the rite was primarily racial, Hebrew-Christians may observe it if they like, in order to maintain their racial connexion with the rest of the Jewish nation. For they still have a strong national feeling, and, indeed, as recent events in Germany have shown us, they are still sometimes regarded as Jews by their Gentile fellow-Christians.[1] Yet, however keen may be their desire to be regarded as Jews, and to be given a legal position as Jews, throughout the Christian centuries, it has been found impossible in practice Those who have tried it have invariably either gone back to Judaism pure and simple, or have ceased to observe Jewish rites, and so have become ordinary Christians.

Thus the combination of Jewish customs and Christian doctrines has never yet worked satisfactorily, even though it has endeavoured to take the form of "a Hebrew-Christian Church." One reason may be that the Jews have had no fixed home. An Indian Christian Church is possible in India, where the converts have always lived. But for the Jews! Heretofore Jewish converts have always necessarily lived among Gentiles (for no Jew will employ a convert or even an enquirer), and have gradually become merged in one Christian body or another. Possibly when Palestine is once more the land of Israel, converts may be able still to live there and practice some

Jewish rites. But he must be of a very optimistic turn of mind who expects that they will ever be recognized as Jews by their unconverted neighbours.[2] Jews are far too irritated with "apostates" for that ever to happen

Yet the practical difficulty of observing Circumcision is not the real reason why the Church has opposed it. Rightly or wrongly, and we believe rightly, Circumcision has stood for the solemn initiation into the religion of Judaism, even more than into its nationality Circumcision is virtually a pledge to follow the Law and obey its enactments. How then can a Christian observe it, in himself or in his children?[3] As a religious rite, and this cannot be separated from its bearing on nationality, it is therefore intolerable to us. We Christians cannot have anything to do with Circumcision. We as Christian people have no national sign at all, and for religious initiation we have Baptism, the symbolism of which precisely answers to our Faith.[4]

There is another fact too about Circumcision which is of some interest. It is not necessary to true religion even on the showing of the Law itself For it was not prescribed to Abraham in Ur of the Chaldees, when he believed God and trusted Him, and followed Him whither he himself knew not. Nor was it ordered even directly he came into the Holy Land, nor even immediately after he had come back into it from the South Country and Egypt. Nor was it commanded even immediately after the patriarch's courageous rescue of Lot, and his dedication of the tenth of the spoils to Melchizedek, and his self-denying refusal to take any reward from the godless king of Sodom.

Ten years passed by between the return from Egypt and the birth of Ishmael, and yet another thirteen before God bade Abraham and his descendants be circumcised (Gen xvi. 3, 16; xvii. 1, 10). It is not the case, that is to say, that Circumcision was all-important, and that complete faith and trust followed upon obedience to that enactment. The facts are in the reverse order. First, faith, and then Circumcision. In the abstract, therefore, the rite cannot be necessary to faith, and whatever may be its value as a national rite (and we are not now concerned with that) it is not indispensable for religion, no, not even for those who wish to be the true children of Abraham, for faith comes first (*cf.* Rom. iv. 9–12).

(2) *The Sabbath.*

The reasons for Christians ceasing to observe the Sabbath run on much the same lines, though there is less objection to keeping the Sabbath than there is to performing Circumcision.

The Lord Jesus indeed recognized the existence of the Sabbath, but He insisted that the principle of its inferiority to Circumcision should be extended [5] It was not to be the iron cast statute that the Jews had made it. Not, it may be noted, that popular language has been right in saying that the Jews find the Sabbath a dull day. This is to misunderstand the relation of Jews to the Sabbath. With them it is a day of happiness and joy. They get far more enjoyment out of their Sabbath day of rest than many Christians get on their Sunday.[6]

Yet the reason for the change of the weekly day

of rest in Christian countries from the Saturday to the Sunday has nothing to do with the comparative happiness of the two days in the experience of those who observe them.

Neither is it a matter of formal rule. The Lord Jesus never "changed the day." Nor did the Apostles. Nor indeed did the early Christians ever meet in council and formally abrogate the Saturday and substitute the Sunday. It was not a matter of formal decision at all. For, among other reasons, anything of the nature of such a binding decision would be contrary to the spirit of Christianity, which, properly speaking, knows nothing of formal enactments binding on the Church. Such enactments belong to times when the nature of the Faith was becoming obscured by the tendency of human nature to take the easy way of obedience to rules, instead of the far more difficult method of keeping in touch with Christ Himself, and therefore of being guided even in details in accordance with His will. The observance of Sunday instead of Saturday is no matter of Christian regulation.

How then came it about? Gradually and quite naturally. The Lord Jesus rose (so all Christians have always held) on "the first day of the week," *i.e.* on the day we now call Sunday, and this was so epoch-making an event, so glorious to the individual believer, and so far-reaching in its issues, that His followers kept the day week by week, with special assemblies in regular commemoration of His resurrection. At first, no doubt, Jewish Christians observed both days, but gradually the significance of "the Lord's Day," *i.e.* the

Sunday, was seen by them to be of so much greater importance than the Sabbath, that, as it was very difficult to keep both days, little by little the Sunday alone was observed, and the Saturday neglected.

"But this was contrary to the ordinance of God," cries the Jew! Why not? replies the Christian. We are, as has already been shown, no longer under the Law.⁷ We are free to do that which glorifies God and furthers His cause

No command in the Old Testament or in the New binds us because it is a commandment. The Ten Commandments, including the Fourth Commandment about the Sabbath, are not binding as commandments. But we observe them with all our heart and soul in so far as they show us the permanent will of God, leading us forward in His way. But we all share in the horror expressed by St. Paul when he says, *Ye observe days, and months, and seasons, and years* (Gal. iv. 10). Study also his other words: *Let no man judge you in meat, or in drink, or in respect of a feast day or a new moon or a sabbath day . . . if ye died with Christ from the rudiments of the world, why, as though living in the world, do ye subject yourselves to ordinances?* (Col. ii. 16, 20). Observe that these quotations are not adduced here as claiming our obedience, but only as showing the true spirit of primitive Christianity. We have not exchanged the Law of the Old Testament times for a new Law. The so-called "Law" of the Gospel is not Law in the same sense as the rules and enactments in the Law of Moses. It is rather the great principle of Love to God and man in which everything good is summed up (Rom. xiii. 8, 10; *cf.* John xiv. 15).

(3) *The Dietary Laws.*

The *raison d'être* of the Christian's disregard of these will have been seen already, especially in the quotations of the last page or two But the subject must be considered by itself, if only very briefly.

Frankly, it would probably have been a good thing for the health of the nations if the dietary laws, and indeed the sanitary outlook in general of the Mosaic Legislation had been followed by the Christian Church. For there is no doubt that they have made an important contribution to the influences that have maintained the nation of the Jews in being, during the many centuries of their oppression. For, in spite of being herded together, often in the most unhealthy parts of very unsanitary medieval towns, not being permitted to live in country places and there enjoy even that spare amount of fresh air which Christians allowed themselves to breathe, they have, in general, been more healthy than their neighbours, and have often survived where these have died. For this, it can hardly be doubted, the dietary laws have been largely responsible.

I do not make the claim that all these laws had health as their immediate object, or that all were ultimately due to reasons of hygiene either perceived by Moses, or determined by God. So far as we know, this was not the case. Many of the prohibited foods were unwholesome, particularly in a hot climate. But others were often used in the worship of heathen deities

This is no place, however, for discussing the reasons

for their prohibition of certain foods. What we are asking is, Why the Christians disregarded these prohibitions, and did not accept them (no, not even for Hebrew-Christians) as the normal part of practical religious life. The answer is that the same reasons held good as with Circumcision, Sabbath and the Mosaic Law in general. The Christian man is not under regulations and laws.

In the case of the dietary laws, however, including abstinence from partaking of the blood of animals, something more must be said. For the First Council of early Christians which was held in Jerusalem in A.D. 49, when discussing the question of Circumcision and the Law in general, gave the express advice that besides flagrant participation in heathenism only certain forms of food should be avoided by Gentile believers, out of respect (it would seem) to the feelings of their Hebrew fellow-Christians.[8] Yet even though it is there said, *It seemed good to the Holy Spirit and to us to lay on you no other burden, etc.*, even so the advice was never considered to be a binding regulation, which for followers of the Lord Jesus had the force of law.[9] Christians have always been left free as individuals to eat and drink as they think will best tend in their own case to the glory of God and the service of man.[10]

Chapter XIV.

QUESTIONS ABOUT CERTAIN CHRISTIAN RITES.

THIS book would hardly be complete if it did not attempt to answer some enquiries about well-known customs of Church order which are not at once intelligible to non-Christians.

For example, why do Christians insist on Baptism, and what precisely does it mean?

Jews should be the last people to ask why we insist on Baptism, for they themselves regard it as all-important. I mean that they allow a Jew to hold any opinions he likes, even to acknowledging the supremacy, and, I presume, even the Divinity, of Christ, but, so long as he does not exhibit his belief to the whole world by the overt act of being baptized, they treat him as a Jew, and at his death claim his body for Jewish burial But let him be baptized! Then, even though his opinions may be quite unsatisfactory from a Christian point of view, they reckon him as an apostate from the Jewish faith, and will have no more to do with him, save perhaps (for a short time) to offer him every inducement in their power to return to them.

In other words, the importance of Baptism as an open test of faith in Jesus is acknowledged by both sides. Jews say: if a man is not baptized he is still a Jew, whatever he may profess to think. Christians say: if the man's faith in Christ is heartfelt faith, he will gladly express that faith of his in public confession even at the cost of leaving his former co-religionists, and often, his dearest friends. Hence all Christians insist on those who profess to believe in Jesus being publicly baptized.

"All Christians," I have said. For it is so with two notable exceptions; the Salvation Army and the Friends (Quakers). But even here the exception is more of form than of reality. For the essence of Baptism is publicity, and a man who refuses public profession of his new faith is not worth having. Such publicity is afforded in almost every meeting of the Salvation Army. Members of that association are not allowed to hide their light under a bushel.

What then of the Quakers? They are excellent and godly Christians who represent a reaction against too much observance of forms, and carry out their opinions as far as possible. But here also they have the essence of Baptism. For no one can accuse Quakers of shrinking from open profession! To be a Quaker has always meant public confession of faith in Christ, and conscientious obedience to His will

The other part of the question demands a few words. What does the form of Baptism precisely mean? For, like all religious rites, it is symbolic. In them something more than the mere act is always implied. What implication underlies the symbol in the case of Baptism? Open profession, of course, but that lies in the act itself. What else is there?

Water cleanses. To be under water for more than a very short time brings death. To rise up out of it suggests restoration to life. Baptism is a representation of all this. As water cleans the body, so Baptism cleans the soul. And, further, the suggestion is that the person baptized goes quite under the water, as a picture of dying to the world and all that is in it. Then the rising up from the water suggests life of a new and fresh kind.

Yet two or three questions may here occur to the reader.

Is this marvellous change in a person produced invariably? A very natural question, but from the point of view of the Christian rather a foolish one. For the Christianity of the New Testament, and with that alone are we concerned, knows nothing of any spiritual result being invariably bound up with any external action. The heartfelt assent of the individual is taken for granted, but if there is none, and the act be performed as a mere performance, no result takes place.

But someone may say that St. Paul writes: *Buried with Him (i.e. Christ) in Baptism, wherein ye were also raised with Him* (Col. ii. 12). Yes, and St. Paul is right. For that is the effect of Baptism. It is the culminating point, the very apex, of faith in Christ, and with it the believer receives all that is implied in becoming a true Christian, including union with Christ and increasing likeness to Him.

Again, it may be asked whether the form of Baptism by total immersion is always carried out?

The answer is that it was the form St. Paul had in mind, but that probably it has never been considered absolutely necessary, even in the first century.[1]

Yet even to-day it is still the norm of Baptism. In the rite of the Greek Church all infants are completely immersed, and in the English Book of Common Prayer total immersion is regarded as the regular method. But if parents inform the minister that the child is delicate, it suffices to pour water on it. Hence it is that there are in England many baptismal fonts which are quite large enough to allow a child to be immersed. But in practice it is found that parents always think that in the cold English climate it is too dangerous for their babies to be dipped in the water, so that unless special request be made, the clergyman assumes that the child will be baptized by affusion. He is, however, always exceedingly careful to use plenty of water.[2]

We now come to the only other Sacrament which the Lord Jesus is related to have bidden His followers observe, the Sacrament of the Lord's Supper, or the Holy Communion, or the Eucharist, as it is sometimes called. Now it might have been supposed that this is outside our purview in this book. For the Lord's Supper has nothing to do with Jews or other non-Christians. It is for Christians, convinced and professing Christians only. Yet Jews live among Christians, and read Christian newspapers, and even sometimes enter Christian churches, not indeed as worshippers, but as sightseers, and they cannot but hear and see things connected with this Sacrament. And, in consequence, they cannot help wondering about it, and desiring an explanation of many things concerning it.

Why was it instituted? Briefly, to remind Christian people of Christ's death for them; to be a special

THE SACRAMENTS: THE LORD'S SUPPER

bond between Christians, a kind of family feast, and also to be a special means of communion with Him who, as Christians believe, is still alive, though unseen, and does impart life to them

Now it must not be supposed for a moment that I intend discussing or stating in any detail the Christian doctrine of the Holy Communion beyond what is contained in the summary just given. This is not the place. It is sufficient to say that at His last meal with His followers before His crucifixion the Lord Jesus took bread and wine (the two common elements of the daily food), and reminding them, as it were, of the paschal lamb which was to be offered next day, called the bread His Body and the wine His Blood, bidding His followers eat and drink them as representing the new covenant which He was inaugurating for them. This they have done ever since that day, and the observance of the Sacrament has always been the most solemn religious service held by Christians.

Perhaps the reader will ask me what I think of this or that interpretation given to the Sacrament by various parts of the Christian Church? This is hardly necessary when I add that I am a clergyman of the Church of England, and have taken on four or five occasions the solemn oath not to use in church any other prayers than those contained in the Book of Common Prayer—"except so far as shall be ordered by lawful authority." Under the same solemn oath I assented to the Thirty-nine Articles of the Church of England. No one who takes these oaths conscientiously, and keeps them, can go very far wrong in his interpretation of the rite. Saying this, it is unnecessary to do more than point out that doctrines and practices which are not contemplated in the Book of Common Prayer or in the Thirty-nine Articles, are not part of the teaching of the New Testament—the one standard of the Church of England—and therefore need not be seriously considered by anyone who wishes to make up his mind whether to be a Jew or a Christian.

There is one other matter. It is not uncommonly asserted that an enquirer is often troubled by the question which body of Christians he should join. Frankly, I cannot be expected to give a quite unbiassed answer. For as a clergyman of the Church of England (as I have just said) I naturally believe her doctrines to approach more closely to the teaching of the New Testament than do those of any other body. But, allowing for that, an enquirer will do well to join himself to that body of Christians with which he happens to be brought in closest contact. Yet he will remember also that one is admitted by Baptism primarily not to the fellowship of a particular body— a "Church," as it is called—but to the great company of all believers, the Church, the whole Body of Christ. *Ye are come*, says the author of the Epistle to the Hebrews, *unto Mount Zion, and unto the city of the living God, the heavenly Jerusalem, and to innumerable hosts of angels, to the general assembly and church of the first-born who are enrolled in heaven, and to God the Judge of all, and to spirits of just men made perfect, and to Jesus the mediator of a new covenant* (xii. 22–24).

Come there, Brother, with us.

APPENDIX A.

ST. PAUL.

THE aim of this book is to present to Jews and others our Lord Jesus of Nazareth as the Christ, and to answer some difficulties that they may feel about both Him and the effect of believing on Him. Strictly speaking, therefore, it is not necessary to say anything about St. Paul.

Yet at least Jews will expect me to say something. For they often write of St. Paul as the *vera causa* of historical Christianity as we know it. They say that Jesus of Nazareth was a pious—a very pious—young man who desired to reform the Judaism of His time, and was for this reason so opposed by the leading Jews that they finally rejected Him as the Messiah, and further, that the Romans were so suspicious of Him that they—not the Jews—put Him to death, and that that was the end of Him.

Strangely enough, however, Saul of Tarsus somehow became convinced that Jesus was, after all, the Messiah, and was actually in heaven, whence He had spoken to him on the Damascus road. Further, this Saul, a Jew of some education and even of some training in Greek thought, evolved a system of belief, in any case strongly anti-Jewish, and derived, it is said, from the Oriental-Greek mysteries of the day, to the effect that God had taken human nature in Jesus of Nazareth and had lived on earth, and after death, had returned to heaven. Further, that men as sinners needed the salvation which such a God-man could secure.

But, that St. Paul, as the Christians call him, was ever much read in rabbinic lore, as Christians foolishly suppose, or had had at any time a deep acquaintance with Judaism in its true character and spirit, modern Jews eagerly deny. For how, they ask, could St Paul the Jew have spoken of the Law as he did.[1]

To take this last point first. St. Paul, the Jew, they say could not write of the Law as disparagingly as he did.

Quite so. No Jew as such could have written thus. But why not, if he had already become a convert to Christ? Is it such an unheard of thing that those who leave their religion speak very strongly of the faults they have found in it? While that very learned Jew, R. Solomon ha Levi (A.D. 1350–1435) was still a Jew, he defended Judaism with all his might. But when he became a Christian and was known as Paul of Burgos he found bitter fault with his former religion.

Observe that I am not defending for a moment the Bishop of Burgos' persecution of his former co-religionists. Such an act was wholly in the decadent spirit of the time. It was long before the days of the boasted tolerance of the nineteenth century, which itself, in so far as it was not based on true religion, has proved to be illusory and fleeting. The fourteenth and fifteenth centuries were not even like our own time. Force was held to be the best way of winning other people to the Gospel of Love. I do not whitewash Paul of Burgos' actions in the least. Nor would I place him for a moment on intellectual or spiritual equality with the great saint whose name he adopted. I only say that although Paul of Burgos had been a very learned and famous Rabbi, he yet could speak very strongly indeed against the Law of Moses as such. We therefore cannot be surprised that he who is said to have sat at the feet of Gamaliel should insist on the weakness of the Law as a means of salvation.

Not, I should suppose, that he came to this knowledge—this perception of the nature of the Law—immediately.

APPENDIX A: ST. PAUL

No doubt he heard Stephen's speech, which had brought out the rebellious character of the Jews to that God who again and again had done so much for them. He had listened to Stephen's words about Jesus of Nazareth, and, as it seems, about part of the ultimate effect of His teaching. But that speech dealt with history, not doctrine, and at most prepared Saul for the acceptance of Jesus as his Leader and Captain. It was this, and (as it would seem) not much more than this which Saul accepted at his "conversion," and in his earliest zeal at once proclaimed in the synagogues at Damascus.

But then followed two quiet and lonely years in Arabia (Gal. i. 17), years that bore some likeness to the forty days temptation of the Master—when he had time to think out matters, and explore the relations and implications of the message of Jesus to all that he had learned in the Rabbinic schools. Then, and not before, he began to grasp the true significance of the Life and Death of Jesus, and of His perfected Life in heaven. Then, and not before, as St. Paul meditated on the needs of his own heart, he recalled the failure of the Law to give him that peace which he now had found in Jesus. And he came to the conclusion—and like Luther, he "could do no other"—that the Law was never meant to be more than a guide to Christ, because of its inherent weakness to give spiritual power over sin and Satan.

If this be so, can we wonder that the man came to grasp the significance of the work, and thus the very nature, of the Christ more clearly, more fully, and altogether more satisfactorily than the honest, but far less educated, fishermen of the Sea of Galilee? They had their part, a very glorious part, in witnessing for Jesus, but to Saul of Tarsus was reserved the greater glory of passing through the deep waters of losing all—in reputation and probably in wealth—for Christ, and of coming into the brighter light of fuller knowledge than they, and so of placing Jesus of Nazareth on a higher and more secure pedestal than had entered at first into their simple and untrained minds.

Yet what St. Paul taught was not new in itself. It was but the logical deduction from the Life of Jesus of Nazareth, including His actions, teaching, death and resurrection.

Jesus, he rightly said, took *the form of a servant, being made in the likeness of men; and being found in fashion as a man, He humbled Himself, becoming obedient* (to God) *even unto death, yea, the death of the cross. Wherefore also God highly exalted Him, and gave unto Him the name which is above every name; that in the name of Jesus every knee would bow, of things in heaven and things on earth and things under the earth, and that every tongue should confess that Jesus Christ is Lord, to the glory of God the Father* (Phil. ii. 7–11).

APPENDIX B.

JEW or CHRISTIAN

JEWS sometimes express the hope that the time is coming when Jews and Christians will combine to form one religion, containing the best parts of Judaism and of Christianity. Nothing, they assert, is more desirable, and, they add, nothing is more probable in the course of time.

But to the present writer nothing seems more improbable, nothing more undesirable.

For how can an amalgam be formed out of the two religions? We grant at once that they have much in common, as, for example, faith in the unity of God (in spite of misunderstandings), belief in the universal spiritual failure of men—with, to some degree at least, the condemnation of all; a common Bible, though Christians call it the Old Testament, a strong belief in prayer and the providential care by the Lord of each one of His servants.

Surely, it may be said, this is enough wherewith to frame a common religion. Is this so? What of the grave differences? One God indeed there is, but to Christians He is no hard arithmetical "One," but Life containing in Himself a threefold "personality." All men have failed indeed, but sin according to Christian teaching is far more deeply rooted in present human nature than it is according to Judaism. The New Testament is a vital part of Christianity which no Jew can accept and no Christian neglect. Prayer and Providential care alone remain, but are not sufficient to be a common religion.

But, further, it may fairly be argued that in reality no two religions are more contrary to each other than Judaism and Christianity. It is indeed true that a sense of personal unworthiness to receive God's grace has ever marked the more saintly among the Jews, based in no slight degree on the cry of Psalm cxxxix, and on Abraham's recognition that he is but dust and ashes (Gen. xviii. 27; *cf.* Job xlii. 1-6).[1] But, in spite of this, Judaism, as portrayed in its semi-official writings, with its meticulous weighing of good and evil actions, is essentially piety that would rise from man towards God.[2] Christianity, on the contrary, is a reception, with bare and empty hands, of the love and mercy that God gives. The two doctrines are incompatible, and because Christ preached the latter He was, and is, rejected by most Jews, and accepted with joyful gratitude by Christians.

NOTES.

CHAPTER I.

(1) p. 1. *The LORD*. In deference to the susceptibilities of my Jewish readers I have retained throughout this book this ancient Jewish surrogate for the proper name of the God of Israel, the "Tetragrammaton." I myself have no doubt that this was really pronounced JāHÔH, a name which was accorded to God in remote heathen times. Originally indeed it was JāHÔ, as in fact it occurs by itself in many non-Jewish documents about the beginning of our era. It is also found at the end of many Hebrew names in the Old Testament, though vocalized to Jāhû out of reverence. Thus Elijah's name is in Hebrew: Elijahu ("JāHÔ is my God"). It occurs also at the beginning of Hebrew names, when, in accordance with Hebrew euphony, the first vowel, or even all the first syllable, is condensed. Thus we have Jehoash, Joash ("Jāhô is strong").

But by the time that God revealed it to Moses as the name by which He was to be known to Israel it had already acquired the additional H, making it JāHÔH. This addition was probably honorific, suggesting that the pronunciation of the syllable should be prolonged, particularly in worship. This, by the by, may be the explanation of the curious addition of the H in "Abraham," and of the change to H from Y in "Sarah" (Gen. xvii. 5, 15).

For the pronunciation JăHVéH there is very little evidence, and its spread to-day down to boys' and girls' school books is one of the curiosities of literature. Theodoret (*c.* A.D. 458) indeed tells us that the

150   THE FOUNDATION OF THE CHRISTIAN FAITH

Samaritans said *Yabe* and the Jews *Aia*, but there is some doubt even about this as a fact, and in reality JăHVéH is little more than a mistaken deduction made by Ewald in the middle of the nineteenth century from Exod. iii. 14 *seq.*; vi 2 *seq* It explains none of the Hebrew proper names. Least of all could its two quite short vowels be used in the loud call upon the Deity in the customary worship of Israel. See for fuller information my article in the *Journal of Theological Studies*, XXVIII (1927), pp. 276 *sqq.* and Dr. F. C. Burkitt's, pp. 407 *seq.*

(2) p. 2. *Jew. Enc.*, i. 86.

(3) p. 4. Prof. Gerhard Kittel indeed complains of the deterioration of Germans by the influx of Jews. It is not evident to foreigners. See Prof. Gerhard Kittel's *Die Judenfrage*, 1933, pp. 21 *sqq.*

(4) p. 4. It is of no importance for our purpose whether the words be translated *shall be blessed*, or *shall bless themselves*, *i.e.* congratulate themselves and each other on the privilege of serving the LORD. If, however, the reflexive meaning be given, and if the phrase be also understood in the sense that the Gentiles (whether they worship the LORD or not) take the prosperity of Abraham's descendants as their ideal of blessing, the argument above is not weakened in any way.

Chapter II.

(1) p. 8. See Dr. A. Ruppin, *The Jews in the Modern World*, 1934, p. 27.

(2) p. 11. Achad Ha'am (Asher Ginzberg) died in 1926. See his works, almost *passim*, *e.g.* Leon Simon's translation, 1922, pp. 25 *seq.*

NOTES 151

(3) p. 13. Josephus' remarks bear out the character of John. See *Antt.* xv, XVIII. v. 2 §§ 116–119. On that passage and on the possible genuineness of the Slavonic variations, see H. St. John Thackeray, *Josephus, the Man and the Historian*, 1929, pp. 131–133, 151; Foakes Jackson, *Josephus and the Jews*, 1930, pp. 279–283.

(4) p. 14. See page 61, note 4.

CHAPTER III.

(1) p. 20. ? Ruysbroeck.
(2) p. 24. See Chapter VII.
(3) p. 25. One of the worst examples is the "proof" of the Perpetual Virginity of the Blessed Virgin Mary found in the *Porta clausa* of Ezek. xliv. 2. See Rufinus (c. A.D. 390) *On the Apostles' Creed*, § 9.
(4) p. 25. "The revelation, howsoever received, they spoke out in human language, for the most part in sober reasoned utterances. The words heard by the people were not always the very sayings of God, if for no other reason than that they passed through the prophets' own consciousness, and of course it was not possible for these men to rise entirely above its limitations But the great prophets were true 'men of God,' mediators between God and His world. God was communicating His will unto Israel as unto no other nation. As through neither Greek philosopher nor poet He *spoke in the prophets.* And it is a fact that the religious man of to-day, opening the pages of the prophets, with and without 'Thus saith the Lord,' and reading with spiritual discrimination, can hear the very words of God to his soul. The religious consciousness of every age *reacts* to such words, and

they are found to be from above. They are life-giving because, in essence, they are from God Himself."
R. S. Cripps, B.D., *A Critical and Exegetical Commentary on the Book of Amos*, 1929, pp. 81, *seq.*

(5) p. 26. In spite of the accidental anagram in *vv.* 1, 2, 3, 4, SiM'oN (Simeon), said by many scholars to refer to Simon the Maccabean High Priest, 141 B.C.

(6) p. 27. It is a moot point whether the Lord Jesus on the Cross did not recall the tenour of the whole Psalm, though the evangelist mentions only its opening words.

(7) p. 27. *Vide infra*, Chapter XII, p. 117.

Chapter IV.

(1) p. 33. See Chapter VII, p. 56.

(2) p. 33. Some Jewish polemical writers have professed to believe that, unless the author of a New Testament book is known by name, its statements are worthless as evidence. Yet surely a Jew should be the last of all people to say this! For who wrote the Law? It nowhere claims to be written by Moses. Who wrote the Book of Joshua? It never says that the author was Joshua. Who wrote Judges or Samuel, or Kings or even Ruth or Chronicles? And who wrote the Book of Job, or the greater part of the Psalms, or even the Second and Third parts of Isaiah, and the second half of Zechariah? And who was the nameless writer who produced the Book that foretold the coming of "My Messenger," a term which in Hebrew is "Malachi"?

I cannot think that any educated Jew will say that mere "tradition" is sufficient to prove authorship with any noticeable degree of certainty. The writings of the New Testament are at least far better off for probability of authorship than those of the Old.

NOTES

I need not waste time in discussing the absurd statement that the New Testament was composed in the days of Constantine. See my *Short Introduction to the New Testament for Jewish Readers*, Edinburgh House, London, 1920.

(3) p. 35. See Strack, *Jesus, die Häretiker und die Christen*, 1910.

CHAPTER V.

(1) p. 40. Sir Owen Seaman, *War Time Verses*, 1915, p. 8.
(2) p. 43. A. Edersheim, *The Life and Times of Jesus the Messiah*, 1883.
(3) p. 43. F. W. Farrar, *The Life of Christ*, 1874.
(4) p. 43. Jos. Klausner, *Jesus of Nazareth* (Modern Hebrew), 1922; English Translation, 1928.
(5) p. 43. Charles Gore, *Jesus of Nazareth*, 1929.

CHAPTER VI.

(1) p. 45. Mark xi. 15–18; *cf.* John ii. 15. Superficial writers assert that Jesus here used "force," and some pretend to see even traces of vindictiveness.

CHAPTER VII.

(1) p. 57. T. B. *Berakoth*, 14b, 15a. For other passages see especially Mishna *Berakoth* II. 2; T. B. *Berakoth* 13b; *Mechilta*, Exod. xx. 2; *Siphra*, Lev. xx. 26. *Cf.* also Wisd. x. 10.
(2) p. 57. *Some Aspects of Rabbinic Theology*, 1909, pp. 66 *seq*.
(3) p. 58. The exception is the *Midrash Breshith ha-Gadol*, perhaps compiled by Moses ha-Darshan, who lived in the eleventh century, and quoted for us only in Ramon Martini's *Pugio Fidei*, Edn. 1687, p. 397. Martini, a

154 THE FOUNDATION OF THE CHRISTIAN FAITH

Spanish Dominican Friar, died at some date after A.D. 1284. For the genuineness of Martini's quotations see my article on "The Jews· Christian Apologists in Spain," in the *Church Quarterly Review*, 1926, p. 108.

(4) p. 61. The Lord Jesus never called any of the leaders hypocrites in our meaning of the word. For there is no evidence that the Greek word so transliterated was ever used at that date in a worse sense than *play-actor*. The Pharisees did, no doubt, "put their goods in the window," but the goods were real so far as they went. See my *Talmudic Judaism and Christianity*, 1933, pp. 66–76.

(5) p. 62. Quoted from the *Philosophy of Right*, § 258, by Hetherington and Muirhead, *Social Purpose, a Contribution to a Philosophy of Civic Society*, 1918, p. 93.

(6) p. 63. For example, his attitude to Gentiles, Acts x. 1–xi. 18. There seems, it may be added, to be no bridge, or any historical connexion whatever, between the promise to St. Peter and the exclusive claim to him on the part of the Roman branch of the Catholic Church.

(7) p. 64. Bishop Robertson's Bampton Lectures, *Regnum Dei*, 1908, pp. 281, 368.

(8) p. 64. "When the Norman bishops asked Anselm whether Alfege, who was killed by the Danes at Greenwich, could be called a martyr, because he died not on behalf of the faith of Christ, but only to prevent the levying of an unjust tax, Anselm answered—'He was a martyr, because he died for justice; justice is the essence of Christ, even though His name is not mentioned'." (Dean Stanley, *Christian Institutions*, 1881, p. 39.)

(9) p. 64. Quoted from *Ethics*, IV, xviii. Schol., by Hetherington and Muirhead, *op. cit.*, p. 141.

NOTES 155

(10) p. 65. *Ibid*, p. 260.
(11) p. 65. *Prometheus Unbound*, Act iv. 570–579.
(12) p. 66. Prof. J. Iverach, *Enc. of Relig. and Ethics*, i. 356.
(13) p. 67. Sanday in Hastings, *D. B.* ii. 621.
(14) p. 67 *Vide supra*, p. 41.

CHAPTER VIII.

(1) p. 71. There is, indeed, some slight evidence that John was put to death with his brother James by Herod Agrippa I in A.D. 44 (Acts xii. 2), but it is too late (Philip Sidetes, fifth century) to be accepted in view of the positive statement of Irenaeus (*c.* A D. 180). Irenaeus had himself come from Asia Minor, the reported dwelling-place of John in his old age until his death in the days of Trajan (A.D. 98). See Irenaeus, *Haer.* II. xxxiii. 3 [xxii 5]; *cf.* III. iii. 4
(2) p. 72. All Gentile readers of Rashi will remember their delight in the ingenuity of his summary of Midrashic expositions of Gen. 1. 1.
(3) p 73. I am well aware that my intimate friend the late Canon Box, an excellent scholar, held that the *Fragment Targum* used *Memra* in the sense of a separate Divine Being, whose relation to God is not strictly defined. But I cannot think his arguments conclusive. *Cf.* G. F. Moore, *Judaism*, 1927, 1. 417–419; Strack-Billerbeck on John i. 1, 1924; ii. 302–333.
(4) p. 74. Ezekiel's vision of someone like a *Man* on the Throne (i. 26) suggests that the antithesis between God and man may be more apparent then real. Kimchi (*in loco*) is well worth studying. *Cf.* my *Hebrew-Christian Messiah*, pp. 277 *sqq*.
(5) p. 75. On the almost unique use of our Lord's address "My Father," in contrast to "Our Father," see my

156 THE FOUNDATION OF THE CHRISTIAN FAITH

article in the *Journal of Theological Studies*, xxxi. 121 (Oct., 1929), pp. 42-47. Dr. C. G. Montefiore says of it that it "gives a very good summary of the facts," but, naturally, he does not agree with the inferences I draw from them (*Rabbinic Literature and Gospel Teachings*, 1930, p. 129).

(6) p. 75   See Mark i. 35; vi. 46; xiv. 32, 35, 39; Luke iii. 21; ix. 18, 28 *seq.*; xi. 1.

(7) p. 77. The reader is strongly advised to study the Fourth Gospel for himself, without any Commentary. He will notice in particular: v. 19, 26, 30, 43; vi. 35, 37, 40, 57; vii. 28 *seq.*; viii. 38, x. 38; xi. 41, xiv. 9 *seq.*, 23; xvi. 28; xvii. (all).

Chapter IX.

(1) p. 83. By the Rev. A. O. Lukyn-Williams, M.A., Vicar of St. James', Cheltenham. Slightly modified from the original form published by the *Church Missions to Jews*, 1929. I am grateful to the Committee for encouraging its reproduction.

(2) p. 83. From *The Christian Message*, issued by the *Conference of Christian Missions*, 1928.

(3) p. 85. Inge, in *Contentio Veritatis*, 1902, p. 99.

(4) p. 88. Prebendary W. Wilson Cash, *C.M.S. Intercession Paper*, July-September, 1928.

(5) p. 89. *In the Purpose of God*, pp. 81 *seq.*

(6) p. 91. Miss A. M. R. Dobson, *Mount Sinai*, 1925, p. 35.

(7) p. 92. See the *Report of the British and Foreign Bible Society*, 1922-1923.

(8) p. 92. J. M. Neale.

(9) p. 92. *The Way, the Truth, and the Life* (Hulsean Lectures for 1871), 1893, p. 205.

Chapter X.

(1) p. 99   Dr. K. Kohler, *Jewish Theology*, 1918, p. 86. *Cf.* his article on "Christianity" in the *Jewish Enc.*, 1903, iv. 54.

(2) p. 99.   Judaism has no formal "Creed," but Maimonides' *Thirteen Principles* are generally accepted. They are summarized in the hymn *Yigdal* which is recited daily. Both may be found in Singer's *Daily Prayer Book*, 1914, pp. 2, 89 *seq.*, with Israel Abhahams' Annotations.

(3) p. 100.   The Fatherhood of God is perhaps most clearly expressed in the *Abinu, Malkenu* ("Our Father, our King") to be found in Singer, p. 55, but in it the thought of the King leaves a stronger impression on my own mind than that of the Father. In the Lord's Prayer, on the contrary, the thought of God as Father dominates the whole.

In itself, by the by, the Lord's Prayer might have been used in any synagogue, for it contains nothing that is distinctive of Christianity, and a parallel may be found in early Jewish prayers for almost every clause. Yet when it is taken as a whole, no prayer in the Jewish Prayer Book approaches it for conciseness, fulness, and spirituality.

Two other points may be mentioned. It is strange that the Church often recites the Lord's Prayer without a Doxology, which our Lord assumed would always be added, in accordance with Jewish custom. The addition was indeed so common at first in Church usage that a form actually crept into the ecclesiastical text of Matt. vi.

Perhaps stranger still is the fact that the Church of England has neglected the Lord's Prayer as a guide to the order of its Public Worship.

Chapter XI.

(1) p. 109. On Ezek. i. 26, see Note 4 on Chapter VIII, p. 155.
(2) p. 110. See Chapter III, pp. 24 *seq.*
(3) p. 111. The standard book on the subject is by Canon G. H. Box, *The Virgin Birth of Jesus*, 1916.

Chapter XII.

(1) p. 113. T.B. *Sanhedrin*, 90b.
(2) p. 113. T.B. *Makkoth*, 23b. They are given in detail in the *Jewish Enc.*, iv. pp. 181–186. The word *Torah* has for its numerical value 611, only two less than 613.
(3) p. 115. *Vide infra*, Chapter XIII, 3, p. 135.
(4) p. 116. The difference of context will, I hope, serve as an apology for the repetition of some of the thoughts already expressed in Chapter III, pp. 15, *sqq.*
(5) p. 118. For a fuller examination of Jer. xxxi. 31–34, see my *Christian Evidences for Jewish People*, §§ 230–233.
(6) p. 127.
(7) p. 127. "*Wipe away.*" It is well known that the Hebrew word *kippĕr* is ambiguous. It seems that in the early Assyrian–Babylonian language there were two distinct roots, both KPR, the commoner meaning "cleanse," "wipe off," and the rarer meaning "cover." The Hebrew language seems to have taken them both over. For an exhaustive study of the renderings in the Septuagint, see C. H. Dodd, *Journal of Theological Studies*, xxxii. (1931), pp. 352–360.

Chapter XIII.

(1) p 130. A redeeming feature in the German legislation of 1933 is that it is not based on religious but only on racial distinction. In this respect it is better than the earlier laws, which permitted Jews to hold certain positions in Germany only if they became Christians.

(2) p. 131. Christians will watch with the deepest interest Sir Leon Levison's experiment of a Hebrew-Christian Colony near Gaza.

(3) p. 131. St. Paul's words in Gal. v 2, 11 show how early Christians regarded it.

(4) p. 131. On Baptism, *vide*, pp. 139, 160.

(5) p. 132. *Vide supra*, p. 129.

(6) p 132. See my *Talmudic Judaism, etc.*, pp. 53, 56.

(7) p. 134. *Vide supra*, pp. 123 *sqq*.

(8) p. 136. The exact text, and the exact meaning, of Acts xv. 20, 28, 29 are not certain, but the general statement as here given is undisputed.

(9) p. 136. Curiously enough the absence of any reference to the Council by St. Paul in his Epistle to the Galatians when he was urging the non-necessity of Circumcision, has been used as evidence that his Letter was written before the Council was held. As though he would have been likely to have appealed to it! The whole point of his letter was freedom from rules and regulations, the full freedom that there is in Christ. An appeal to the authority of the Council would have stultified his argument.

(10) p. 136 Thus St. Paul says he will gladly eat no flesh at all if to do so will help others. To-day many Christian people are teetotallers for the same reason. Naturally associations of Christians may draw up regulations for their own members (*e.g* Roman

160   THE FOUNDATION OF THE CHRISTIAN FAITH

Catholics), but even this sometimes comes in practice perilously near outraging the primary liberty of believers.

CHAPTER XIV.

(1) p. 139. The symbolic meaning attributed to Christian Baptism by St. Paul (Rom. vi. 3 *seq.*; Col. ii. 12 *seq.*) implies complete immersion ("submersion," as it has been called). But the historical notices in the New Testament are satisfied with affusion only. The question depends a good deal (though not entirely) on how the Jews at that date baptized proselytes and others. Curiously enough this is not absolutely certain, though the practice to-day among Jews of all kinds and in all countries is complete immersion. Much material bearing on the subject is collected by Strack and Billerbeck on Matt. iii. 6, and an interesting discussion may be found in the *Journal of Theological Studies*, xii (1911), pp. 437–445; 609–612; xiii. (1912), pp. 411–414, between Mr. C. F. Rogers denying, and Dr. Israel Abrahams affirming, Jewish full immersion in the first century A.D. In any case it is not easy to see how the 3000 in Acts ii. 41, and the 5000 (or possibly only 2000) in Acts iv. 4, could have been immersed so quickly as is implied. Nor was the Church tradition that of full immersion generally, as may be seen in the earliest pictures of the rite.

The baptism of the gaoler at Philippi (Acts xvi. 25–34) and his household seems to have taken place in the courtyard of the prison, where perhaps there was a large stone bath for washing purposes, or possibly even a small stream. In either case his baptism will have been by affusion, and not by full immersion.

NOTES

The gaoler himself appears to have been a deputy-centurion (*optio carceris*, in the Latin of the famous Codex Bezae, of probably the fifth century), whose social rank would be much the same as that of our sergeant to-day. He would therefore hardly be in a position to have a private bath, such as Roman higher officers would certainly possess. Besides, the narrative, if taken quite strictly, implies that he was baptized before he took St. Paul into his house (Acts xvi. 33).

(2) p. 140. When the present writer enquired of the Bishop of London in 1893 or 1894, he could not hear of any font in the Diocese large enough to allow an adult to be immersed. He understands that since then two or three have been built. See further *The Record*, March 29, 1935, p. 187.

APPENDIX A.

(1) p. 144. See many quotations from Jewish writers in my *Talmudic Judaism and Christianity*, 1933, pp. 59–61.

APPENDIX B.

(1) p. 148. G. F. Moore (*Judaism*, 1927, 1930, i 389–398; iii. 121 *seq.*) gives many examples of the recognition by Israel of God's undeserved mercy.

(2) p. 148. Dr. J. Abelson, Senior Minister of the Great and New Synagogues, Leeds, writes. "There are no sinless saints amongst us. God alone is holy. Man can never be holy. He can *strive* to be holy. That is all. Our striving after holiness is accounted to us as holiness. This is our atonement." (*The Jewish View of Atonement*, in Mr. G. A. Yates' Symposium *In Spirit and in Truth*, 1934, p. 99.)

INDICES

I GENERAL

A
Abelson, Dr J, quoted, 161
Abraham,
  promise to, 1
  promise to, fulfilled, 2.
  promise to,
    the threat also fulfilled, 2.
Arguments have changed, x
Assumptions, ix
Atonement, The, not a vicarious sacrifice by a man, 125 *seq.*

B
Baptism,
  why necessary? 137
  its meaning, 138
  effect, 139
  by immersion, 139
  How was the gaoler at Philippi baptized? 160 *seq*
  Jewish usage, 160
Beginning, The, its many interpretations, 72

C
Caviare, May Jews eat? 114
Church, The,
  in what sense necessary, 62
Church, A Hebrew-Christian-, 130
Circumcision, 128
  the Law shows it is not necessary to true religion, 131
Commandments (613), 113
Council of Jerusalem, its decision not binding as law, 136
Creed, Judaism has no formal C, 157

D
Dietary Laws, The, their value, 135.

F
Fatherhood of God in Jewish writings, 157
"Father, My," almost unique use by our Lord, 155 *seq.*

G
Galatians, Ep to, 159
Germany,
  its capital saved by Christianity, 9
  her inferiority-complex gone, 11
God,
  His proper Name, 149.
  the Jewish doctrine, 99
  the Christian doctrine, 100
Gospel, The,
  its central message, 125, *seq*
  not a formula but a Person, 89
Gospels, The Three,
  generally trustworthy, ix
  and straightforward, 70
  Fourth Gospel,
    authorship, 71
    the result of long thought, 70

H
Hegel, on the State, 62
Hitler, Herr Adolf, 3, 11
Holy Spirit, the, 77, 104–106
Hort, Dr, quoted, 92

I
Incarnation, the, 107–111
  not God in, but distinct from, a man, 108
Inspiration, 15, 25
  the extent still doubtful, 34
Intellectualism is not spiritual religion, 19, 21.

INDICES

Israel, her present low state, 7.

J
JăHVéH, little evidence for, 149.
Jesus,
- an Aryan! 5
- His Attraction for a believer to-day, 83–93
- His Attraction not chiefly as a teacher, 85.
- His Communion with His Father, 75
- Deity of, How the belief came, 73
- His Human nature not deified in Gospels, 75
- His Life exhibited only in our life, 38.
- His Life exhibited to-day, 41
- His Love in action, 49
- His Miracles, 35
- His Resurrection the cause of full faith, 74
- His Self-sacrifice, 54
- His Strength of character, 44
- His Teaching still up to date, 88
- Jews misunderstand the Christian doctrine, 74
- Literal Imitation insufficient, 39–41
- "Lives" of many kinds, 43
- No Compulsion to faith, 36
- No Nation has taken His life as its standard, 42
- Not Self-absorbed, 46
- the centre of His Teaching, 59
- The Kingdom of Heaven fulfilled in His life, 58
- The Temptation, 51
- Three Traits, 44–55
- Transfiguration, its significance, 53
- What does He tell us about Prayer? 87
- why Rejected? xi, 81 *seq*

Jews, many conversions in spite of persecution, 43.

Jochanan, Rabbi, on the Kingdom of Heaven, 57.
John the Baptist,
- his message, 12 *seq*
- why rejected? xi, 13 *seq*, 29

Judaism cannot be combined with Christianity, 147

K
King, the supreme, not Messiah but God, 58
Kingdom of Heaven, The, 56–68.
- meaning of the phrase, 57
- its principles, 58–62
- fulfilled in life of Jesus, 58
- involves self-sacrifice, 65

KPR, meaning in Hebrew, 158.

L
Law, the,
- Barbaric in parts, 115
- Final reason for its non-observance, its Failure, 123–128
- observed, yet interpreted, by Jesus, 122
- Jews, Inconsistent attitude of some, 115
- no part now binding as "Law," 134
- why not observed by Christians, in general, 112–128
- Spiritual teachings in it intended from the first, 120 *seq*
- the O T itself suggests the supersession of its rules, 116

Life, only from the sacrifice of another's life, 66

LORD, The, the true Name, 149 *seq*

Lord's Prayer, 157

Lord's Supper, the, 140, *seq*

M
Man, the chief end of, 39.

Mark, St, Gospel of, Why used here so much, 50
Memra, 73, 155
Merit, 122
Messiah,
 a natural expectation, 18
 controversy over predictions is avoided, why, 20 *seq*
 how the Church came to find so many "proof-texts" in the Old Testament, 24, 25
 Predictions often uncertain, and not of supreme importance, 22
 Predictions of, not the real basis of faith, 22 *seq*
 Predictions, a few probably real, 26
Miracles, 35
 their evidential value, 36
Moffatt, Dr J, quoted, 84

N

New Testament,
 our study of it independent of inspiration, 34
 uncertainty of authorship no difficulty, 152

O

Old Testament, The
 its high ethical demands from the first, 17
 Christians have followed Jews too closely, 106
 Jews make three divisions with grades of inspiration, 112
 its high value, yet less than NT, 128
 not a verse contradicts the Christian Faith, 104, 106
Oral Law still developing, 114

P

Palestine, a National Home, 7
Palestine, Jewish population to-day, 8
Paul, St, Jewish statements considered, 143–146
"Person," its meaning discussed, 98
Pharisees, not "hypocrites," 14, 154
Pray, the usual word not in Fourth Gospel Why? 75
Prayer, effective, 87.

R

Religion,
 true, due to Abraham's descendants, 4
 the danger of intellectualism in, 19
 must be social, 61
Resurrection of the dead, "proved" from the Law, 113

S

Sabbath, why superseded by Sunday, 132–134
Sacrifices, mistaken opinion that they were not ordered by God, 119
Saints of to-day, viii, 41
Schechter, Dr, on the Kingdom of Heaven, 57
Seaman, Sir Owen, quoted, 40
Sermon on the Mount, is it practical? 67
Shelley, quoted, 65
Son of God, 101–104
Spinoza, quoted, 64.
Spiritual things greater than rules, 29

T

Temple, Arbp W, quoted, 89
Torah, meaning of the word, 113
Trinity, the, 97–106
 not "a compromise with heathenism," 99

V

Virgin Birth, The, 109–111.
Virgin Mary, The, probably the least sinful of all merely human beings, 110

Y

Young thinkers, x.

II BIBLICAL.

	PAGE		PAGE
Gen i 1	72, 155	Matt iv 17	33, 56
Gen xii 1–3	1	Matt v 3	58
Ex xxv 40	120	Matt v 20	61
Ex xxxiii 20	108	Matt v 39	68
Lev. xviii 4 *seq*	124	Matt v 42	67
Deut vi 4	98	Matt vii 1	68
Deut xi 9	113	Matt xvi 18 *seq*	63
I Kings xvii 24	36	Matt xxviii 19	105
Ps ii 7	102	Mark vi 9	41
Ps xxii	27, 152	Mark xi 15–18	153
Ps. xxii 27	117	Mark xii 29	98
Ps xl. 6–8	117	John i 1	72
Ps lxxii	26	John i 4	79
Ps cx	26, 152	John ii 15	153
Isa vii 14	110	John vii 23	129
Isa ix 2–7 (1–6 Heb)	26	John xiv 26	105
Isa lii 13–liii	27	Acts viii 27–35	28
Jer vi 20	29	Acts xv 20, 28, 29	159
Jer xxxi 31–34	118, 122	Acts xvi 25–34	160
Ezek i 26	155	Rom iv 9–12	132
Ezek xliv 2	151	Rom xiii 8, 10	134
Amos v 25	118	Gal v 2, 11	159
Hag ii 11	113		
Matt i 22 seq	110	T B *Berakoth*, 14b, 15a	153
Matt iii 2	33, 56	T B *Sanhedrin*, 90b	113
Matt iv 1	105	T B *Makkoth*, 23b	158